A JOURNEY THROUGH GRACE

A JOURNEY THROUGH GRɑCE

A Memoir

REGGIE TUGGLE

Mynd Matters Publishing
715 Peachtree Street NE
Suites 100 & 200
Atlanta, GA 30308

e-ISBN: 978-1-953307-56-9
ISBN: 978-1-953307-54-5 (pbk)
ISBN: 978-1-953307-55-2 (hdcv)

Author photo courtesy of Glyn A. Stanley

To my Creator, whose sense of imagination is unfathomable. Who could have ever foreseen a car accident would result in my mother being forced to stay in Denver, Colorado where she would finish high school and give birth to me. My mother taught me about life, God, and how to love myself. I owe whatever blessings I have been able to share with others to her teachings and her eternal love.

CONTENTS

INTRODUCTION

The keys to living a complete life is to learn to
balance time, resources, and talent,
by the grace of God.

Over the years, when people heard about the remarkable and extraordinary blessings in my life, they would ask if I plan on placing some of these events in a book. My immediate reaction has always been to feel as though my life isn't worthy of a book. However, upon reflection, I felt like God should be acknowledged for the grace he has given me and the wonderful plans he bestowed upon my life. The following pages are a summary of years of unexplainable and unexpected opportunities that brought unimagined blessings. How did I get to be me? I am more than the composite of all my life experiences. When I say more than my experiences, I am referring to the inner self of spiritual awareness. We also are what we think and feel intuitively.

We have to spend our time in meditation, prayer, and silence, listening for what's happening around us and within. It's subtle, but the messages are clear. When I'm experiencing something new, or what others may consider being "risky," I have found that if it felt right and the comfort level was strong, then it was the correct thing for me to do. I always got into trouble when I tried to take matters into my own hands and force something to happen. I believe God moves us in quiet yet definitive ways. You can't always make blessings happen. Sometimes, you have to be in the places where blessings flow naturally. It's not always what you know, but where you are. It's the time and space you occupy at the "moment." It's not what you know or whom you know, but who knows you. Life is about places and spaces…being in the right place at the appropriate time to have that special conversation with that particular person. I call it serendipity. You can't always plan for it, but you can always be alert and watch for it. When you hear the message or get the feeling, you have to act on it or lose it.

Beginning with my birth to a wise, teenage, unwed mother, to going to college with very little money and the struggles I faced during that time, to my years of international travel, and then, the pursuit of a Ph.D. at Yale University. My life moved forward, and I entered in a new phase of my life as I served as a pastor for thirty-eight years at one church and seeing its membership grow from forty to nearly 1000 members. This led to successfully conducting two capital campaigns for two new church buildings' construction, having some prestigious secular work experiences in higher education, corporate, and political arenas.

Doing all the above is in itself worthy of telling the story of what God has done in my life. But to have been blessed to do all these things while at the same time, living through severe hardships as well as moments, makes the story unbelievable.

I have been blessed time and time again as I grew up in poverty, dealt with my brother's premature death, to the time when I married an exceptional woman who bore two intellectually gifted daughters. Sorrows have also been a vital part of my life as I experienced the death of my wife. But then, I was blessed with a new wife and life partner, and by God's grace, moved to Charlotte, North Carolina to build a new life in retirement.

This book, on the surface, may appear to be about accomplishments and unusual experiences. However, in fact, it is a sincere attempt to put in writing the tangible presence of God's hand upon my life. It's about my escape from misfortune and the adversary's relentless traps to destroy my purpose and my gifts.

My miraculous life started out as a series of unrelated random events and conversations with people over the years. Still, looking retrospectively over the course of my life, I can see God's hand from the very beginning until now. The mystery isn't that I am guided and protected, but my portion of blessings exceeded that of most others. My cups run over.

I sometimes feel uncomfortable because I have been so blessed. So, the question arises, "What am I supposed to do with my life with all these opportunities?" I discovered the answers over a period of time, not all at once, but at the instances when I could appreciate the answers. God wants me to enjoy the gifts on the one hand and then, on the other, to be of service to Him in blessing others as well. And that is how I perceive my life to be.

First and foremost, I am a servant of God. I serve Him, His people, His purpose, and His will. I have been blessed so that my testimony will bring hope and encouragement to those who are going through their own trials and tribulations. I am worthy of all these blessings only in the context of my willingness to help others—to know themselves in relation to the Creator, to know the gospel of salvation, and to value each day, i.e., to maximize their own gifts and potential.

The single most valuable advice I learned over the years when facing difficulties is, "Nothing stays the same forever." Every person on the planet experiences bad times, hard times. The key is to face what's facing you head on without lamenting the fact that it's you who is having the experience. It's never about "why me?" It's about knowing that God has this situation in control and we must do what the situation requires without becoming bitter or cynical. Joy must be the order of the day. Burdens and pain can blind us, if we are not careful. Even when joy may not be obvious every day, we have to remember that we can't let our burdens blind us to the reality of God's hand holding us.

Scripture has other words for this kind of joy—it's called trust in God, as well as trust in your own abilities and resources no matter how meager they seem. God manifests his love for us best in times of adversity when we don't see any way to move forward. When our back is against the wall, and there is no door to open, we will see that we do have resources that can be applied to the moment if we keep moving forward.

I have learned that when we don't give up or give in, God continues to move us forward to higher and greater blessings. We relax during those phases.

Life is work, hard work, and it's unpredictable at best. This isn't new, and it certainly isn't a secret, but it is something many, if not most, people fail to apply. Herein lies the key to life with all of its uncertainties. When we give up too soon, we miss the blessing that's just around the corner. One day at a time. One day at a time. That's all the amount of grace God gives us. Just enough grace for the day, and before we realize it, the day becomes a long line of days which become months, then years, and then, a whole life.

Chapter 1

THE EXPECTATIONS AND THE RESULTS

*We all come from somewhere, and we carry that
place with us wherever we go.*

I have lived four years beyond the promised three scores and ten (Psalm 90). I feel it's time for me to recount my life's story and tell about the remarkable blessings I have known since my birth. In spite of countless obstacles and barriers, trials and tribulations, "God has anointed my head with oil and my cup(s) overflow." I have felt God's hand on my life since I was about nine years of age. I knew it was God and I was being protected for a purpose, not known then, that has been revealed through a series of events and circumstances leading to my growth, spiritually and emotionally.

My life was blessed because, as shall be revealed later, of the extraordinary challenges I faced before leaving home for college. I should have been propelled into a life of failure wrapped in cynicism. Yet, time and time again, I was protected, guided, and pushed by God's grace through doors that seemed to magically open to new opportunities and close on their own when a chapter would end. At first, I was curious, then mystified, then later, much later, expecting. The blessings came mostly in the form of the people God would place in my path, a brief conversation at a restaurant, making a friend of a person I just met at the cafeteria line or sitting next to someone at a fundraising dinner. They came for a season. Deposited a word or a blessing and then disappeared, leaving me with a blessing greater than what I had known before meeting them. I say it was God because life is just too vast and unpredictable for it to have been otherwise.

I learned long ago, without being fully cognizant of it, that it was important to live with great intentionality. In other words, on purpose or with a purpose. And the purpose was always aligned with a specific goal, either stated or unstated. Some goals had an immediate demand on my life, like finishing high school or making sure I earned a specific dollar amount from my summer employment before returning to college in the fall, or making sure I wasn't sidetracked into wasting time. Some days produced forward movement to attain grander blessings, like how to get into seminary, then pursue a Ph.D. or plan to accept my first real job either at the church or in the secular world. I was always thinking about my future and how to prepare for whatever was coming down the road. Preparation was the key. I had to be prepared—academically, emotionally, spiritually, and physically.

* * * *

Over the years, I have been blessed to have many kinds of jobs. My life progression can, in part, be interpreted by the jobs I've held over the years. They, themselves, tell a remarkable story of an unseen hand guiding my life.

- Age 11: swept hair at the local barbershop

- Ages 12 and 13: worked as a caddy at City Park Golf Course

- Age 14: worked for a landscape company

- Age 15: worked as a sacker at Safeway grocery store and by age 22, as an assistant store manager

- Age 22: was a store cashier at a community grocery store in Manhattan

- Age 23: was a waiter at a restaurant in New York and pastor at the Calvary Presbyterian Church in Asbury Park, New Jersey

- Age 23: worked with migrant workers in West Hampton Long Island (summers only)

- Age 24: pastor at the Community Baptist Church, New Haven, Connecticut

- Age 24: adjunct professor at West Haven University, teaching political science

- Age 26: began pastoring at the Memorial Presbyterian Church in Roosevelt, New York (served for 38 years)

- Age 27: appointed to serve as the Executive Director of the Roosevelt Anti-Poverty Agency (18 months)

- Age 28: appointed to serve as President of the Urban League of Long Island (2 years)

- Age 29: appointed to serve as Chief of Staff for Presiding Supervisor for the Town of Hempstead, the largest township in New York State (3 years)

- Age 32: appointed to serve as Director of Public Affairs at Newsday, the Island's largest daily newspaper with a circulation of 600,000 (14 years)

- Age 46: appointed Associate Vice President at Nassau Community College (17 years)

- Age 64: served as interim pastor at the First United Presbyterian Church, Charlotte, North Carolina (4.5 years)

- Age 71: serve as interim pastor at the Grier Heights Presbyterian Church, Charlotte, North Carolina (current)

Surprisingly, even with all of the work experiences in my life, I have only actually applied for one job.

That fact alone is noteworthy.

God has made it so bountiful that the blessings of employment came to me rather than me having to seek them. I turned down more jobs than I accepted. God has blessed me beyond what I could have planned for or imagined.

* * * *

OFF TO SEE THE WORLD

Many people dream of being able to see the world. I never had those dreams per se, but I certainly have been blessed to explore this vast land, and as an added blessing, for much of my travel, I didn't have to pay for it. I'll get to that later, but in great humility, God has blessed me to have traveled to fifty-two countries and forty-one of the fifty states. I have been a traveler since the age of twenty, when I first left the United States to spend one year in Asia at the Central Philippine University in the Philippines. During my stay, I visited Japan, Hong Kong, Thailand, and Taiwan.

God has permitted me to see England (2x), Ghana, Ethiopia, France (2x), Egypt, Panama, Columbia, Israel (7x), Jordan (3x), Vietnam, Cambodia, Uganda, Cuba (3x), Kenya, South Africa, Canada, Mexico (3x), St. Martin (3x), Jamaica (5x), Dominican Republic, Haiti (3x), Russia (2x), Spain, Portugal, Monaco (3x), The Bahamas (5x or 6x), Togo, Dahomey, Aruba, Belgium, France (2x) Austria (2x), Denmark, Sweden, Estonia, Greece, Germany, China, Italy

(3x), St. Thomas, Curacao, Dominica, Puerto Rico (2x), Hong Kong (2x), Thailand (2x), and Singapore. This gives a fair enough idea that I've been blessed to roam around the world.

Chapter 2

LESSONS IN THE ATTIC

*You anoint my head with oil; my cup overflows are
the words found in the last part of Psalm 23. They
certainly apply to my life. My cups overflow.*

Born in 1947 to a teenage mother who had just graduated from high school, my life began in the most unpromising circumstances. For the first nine years, we lived in an attic of a home in Denver, Colorado. It was a small place with two rooms and a bathroom, consisting of only a toilet and sink—no bathtub. In one room, we had a small couch with a small black and white television, and a bed in the other. Our kitchen consisted of only a hotplate next to an old wringer washing machine in the basement. We had no refrigerator and our sink doubled as our place to wash clothes. Yet, my mother was a genius in preparing meals. She could use that hotplate to make fried chicken, pan-fried cornbread, greens, and all kinds of beans. We had white beans, navy beans, pinto beans, black beans, black-eyed peas, butter beans, kidney beans, green beans, pork & beans, and more. We had cornbread just about every day and I loved it. These kinds of foods don't require immediate refrigeration. They could stay out for a day or two and not have to worry about getting spoiled. Sometimes, we had just hot dogs and beans. Saturday mornings were special meals. We had eggs, bacon/sausage, and pancakes.

Since a very early age, I had started making my own breakfast, as my mother had to go to work early. We had just about all of our meals together when she came home from her job at the local cleaners where she was a clothes presser. She hated that job. We'd sit at our small table for two and eat while talking about our day. We'd talk about everything—school, my friends, her job, church, the sermon, and her friends. She told me the circumstances of how she came to Denver as a teenager. Her mother was seriously injured in a car accident while driving from Oklahoma to Denver, resulting in my grandmother having to spend many months recovering. They ended up staying in Denver, where my mother continued her high school education and later gave birth to me.

My mother loved telling jokes and entertained me with endless stories of her childhood growing up in rural Guthrie, Oklahoma, where she was born, one of nine children, in 1928. Other times, when pondering our life in the attic, she'd often tell me that one day she was going to get us a real apartment with a real bathroom and real kitchen. "You'll see, son," she'd say. "God is going to bless us."

She was always concerned about my health, if my shoes fit, and were my shirts fitting okay. Later, as an adult and looking at some old pictures I found, I saw me as a child with some of my neighborhood friends. My clothes were tattered, patches on my jeans, and old sneakers. All of my friends were dressed similarly.

Hmm, I thought to myself. *I never felt poor, deprived, unloved, or unprotected.* I always felt loved and fulfilled.

We were blessed, and I didn't recognize it. **We always had enough; enough joy, enough love, laughter, smiles, enough friends, and enough peace.** Financially, I guess one would say we were poor, but I never knew it.

A lover of crossword puzzles, mother had quite a way with words. She also insisted I bring home A's and nothing less. Of course, I didn't always bring home A's, but I did most of the time. I looked forward to the day when report cards would be handed out. I'd get mine and look to see how many A's I earned because I knew what my reward was. Mother would take me to my favorite chili place and allow me to order a chili-burger with fries at Chris' Diner. At that point in my life, my all-time favorite meal was to eat one of Chris' chili-burgers. We'd walk down to the greasy spoon and have a blast. It was always topped off with her giving me a quarter for every A on my report card. She was my best friend, a blessing I came to recognize many years later.

My mother taught me about life, life events, and life dangers. She'd tell me life doesn't owe me anything and whatever I want in life, I have to get it. Don't expect that anyone is going to give you anything, "If you don't get it, you don't get it." There are so many other gems she taught me.

- Do it right the first time and save time from having to do it again.

- Politeness is a passport around the world.

- It never hurts to be nice.

- You're going places in life young man, be ready.

- You don't have to make an "A" every time, but you do have to do your best all the time.

- Smile, even if you don't feel like it.

- Always put God first in all you do.

- Take God's word seriously.

- Don't follow others, be yourself.

- Always look a person in the eyes when talking to them.

- Always give a firm handshake.

- It's okay to fail, but it's not okay not to try.

- When a person hurts you, leave them to heaven.

- Don't back away from a fight when you must face one, but try not to fight.

- It's not where you've been that defines you, it's where you're going.

- Always be honest; there is no gain in cheating.

- Believe in yourself no matter what your situation or what others say about you. "They ain't paying your bills."

- When it comes to money, give first to God, then to yourself, and save as much as you can.

- Be generous.

- Help others when you can.

- Never give up on yourself.

- Do things others won't even try. Use your imagination as you go through life.

- Always, always, always be yourself.

- You can do anything you put your mind to…

These are just some of the teachings my mother was constantly driving into my head. She was my first teacher, and I didn't recognize her blessing. She didn't preach. She had conversations—casual, gentle, and often entertaining. But the messages were always clear and consistent.

Now, don't get it twisted. I got punished when I did wrong, and I got harsh lectures when I deserved them. She used capital punishment techniques, like an extension cord that would leave welts and a little blood on my backside.

When she finished whipping me, I had to endure her intolerable lectures, which in some aspects, were more painful than the actual beating. She always asked the same question, "Do you know why I whipped you?" I had learned early on that this was a trick question.

If I said no, she'd say, "Oh, you think I'm a mean person who likes beating her son. Is that right?"

If I said I knew why I was being beaten, she'd ask why I disobeyed her. This was another trick question.

If I said I didn't know why I was disobedient or that I didn't remember, she'd say I needed more punishment to help me remember.

If I said I remembered what she said, but disobeyed, I would be regarded as being rebellious and thus need more whippings.

The talk would sometimes last an hour, and I had to sit without looking away or looking as though I was bored stiff. Sometimes, I'd rather just get the physical punishment and get on with my day than to have to sit and listen to her teachings. In my head, I'd be saying, "Enough already, mother, enough!" But of course, I never said that aloud. I love my life too much.

I have been blessed with overflowing cups all of my life, but it began with my mother giving me a sense of self-confidence, a love of adventure, a desire to achieve no matter what others think, to hold fast to values when not experiencing an immediate payoff, how to earn, save, and spend money.

Mother tried to make sure my childhood was well rounded. She placed me in little league baseball and football, gave me clarinet lessons, and pushed me to join the school band and marching band. She wanted me to contact responsible Christian men to counteract the highly dysfunctional life after she got married. More on that later.

THE TALK

I remember preparing to go to college at eighteen. My entire senior year, I waited for "the talk" about what to do, what not to do, and how to behave. I knew she loved to give me advice and teach me about how to do well. But the talk never came. She never sat me down to share her wisdom, fears, and expectations. I waited and waited and waited. Then, as she drove me to the bus station to catch Greyhound to Bishop College in Dallas, Texas, I felt it would be the time. But all she could talk about was how proud she was of me to be the first in our family to go off to college and how much I would be protected by God. As I was about to get on the bus, she grabbed and embraced me and gave me "the talk." **She said, "Son, don't forget who you are."**

That was it. Those six words summarized eighteen years of growing up listening to her teaching and sharing words of wisdom and how important it was to be obedient to the Word of God. If I hadn't learned by then who I was and what I stood for, I'd never know. I didn't know it then, but my mother was an unrecognized blessing. She was the first of many who would come into my life, deposit a blessing, and then disappear.

Chapter 3

WHEN OTHERS HURT YOU, LEAVE THEM TO HEAVEN

My childhood was good for the most part. We didn't have much, materially speaking, but we also didn't want for anything other than necessities. It wasn't until my mother married Walter Parker that my domestic life changed dramatically. My stepfather had two distinct personalities—one when sober and another quite different one when drinking. As a sober man, he worked in a meat processing plant to bring home the bacon (no pun intended).

He dutifully brought home money and handed mother what he felt she needed to pay the bills. Mother was a fantastic money manager. She could stretch President Lincoln's beard so far it would reach his feet. He never gave her too much, just enough to get by. For example, we never went anywhere for fun as a family. We'd never go out to eat at a restaurant.

We ate at greasy spoons where the menus typically included hamburgers, fried chicken, french fries, hotdogs, and chili. But never at a restaurant with tablecloths and a menu handed to you by a waiter. We didn't go to the movies, or to ball games, or picnics. When I went to other places, it was with my mother only or maybe a friend. Our extent of socialization was to visit other people's homes where we'd eat great meals and then sit around, tell stories, and laugh at jokes.

"Drinking Walter" was mean. He was intolerant of almost everything and belligerent. He loved to argue when drunk. He didn't argue to make a point or to offer a better perspective on something. Instead, he'd argue to make you feel bad, to demean, and destroy your will to argue back. And when you tried to argue back, he'd raise his voice and shout and call you ungodly names. He'd get up in your face and dare you to say something different. If you went silent, he'd argue all the more, saying you were disrespecting him, ignoring him, or thinking he was a fool. It was a no-win situation.

"Sober Walter" didn't speak much and was a gentle spirit. He'd even laugh. He had a small gun collection and loved showing them off. It wasn't much, two or three handguns, a couple of rifles, and shotguns. He enjoyed hunting with friends and would often go off for three or five days at a time. He'd bring home a deer or some rabbits. I helped him skin the rabbits and prepared them for the freezer. I got quite skilled in skinning rabbits. I'd sometimes skin and clean fifteen to twenty in one sitting. Deer meat was processed by professionals. He was always proud of his catch.

Drinking Walter would sometimes refuse to give Mother any money at all. She just had to find a way for all of us to make it without his financial contribution that week. If she asked for money, the fight was on. Walter would get very violent when drunk. My mother was an abused spouse. I remember Walter and I having a fistfight while I was a high school senior as I intervened in trying to stop him from hurting her. There came a time when I feared and hated him. The single most important lesson my mother taught me was:

"When a person hurts you, leave them to heaven."
—Romans 12: 17-21

She said that almost every time he hurt her. I knew what she meant, but I didn't want to wait that long. I wanted heaven to intervene NOW.

When I was in seminary, his beating caused Mother to be hospitalized for several days. I plotted a way to fly to Denver, kill him, and return to New York. In those days, one could fly without identification. No one would have suspected me, a seminary student living in New York, I thought. Mother made me promise I wouldn't fly to Denver to see her. It was tough, but I honored her wishes. At the time, however, I thought Walter should be eliminated from the earth, and I was eager to do it.

Sober Walter would show kindness. He'd have a conversation with you, but only if you initiated it. He never once, in all the years they were married, initiated a discussion. I was careful to never mention my wants or accomplishments. He seemed to bristle at hearing about those things. He loved talking about fishing, an activity he didn't invite me to join. Kind, but he never gave more than a smile. He never gave me, or any of us, a Christmas gift, birthday gift, or anything.

Drinking Walter would lash out at anyone in his path. We used to dread him coming home. When his car was pulling into the driveway, we'd all get tense and wonder what was about to come through the door. When I was fourteen, he killed a man in a barroom fight. He got off with five years of probation because of some legal technicality. When I was forty-three, he killed another man in a fight at a gambling den. Both had been drinking when the argument got hot and heavy. The other guy drew a gun, and Walter ran. The other guy fired a shot but missed. Walter got to his truck, where he kept a gun under his seat, grabbed it, turned, and fired back, hitting the man in the chest. He died on the spot before the EMTs arrived.

He was arrested and held overnight and released, claiming self-defense as supported by the testimony of witnesses. He was fined for carrying an unregistered weapon.

Sober Walter was a soft touch for his friends. More than a few times, he'd loan them money. But if Mother asked for some extra cash, one would think she was asking that he give away his gun collection.

Drinking Walter was a man to whom you would never want to be in a position of owing money. If you failed to repay him on the date agreed upon when you borrowed the money, he might give you another date for repayment. But if you missed that date, you had better stay missing and hope you would run into Walter when he was sober. If he was drinking, only God knows what the outcome would be. He didn't mind fighting or, as he would say, "go upside your f____ head."

Later, many years later, when I was in my late thirties, I understood my stepfather better. That, I came to understand, was what my mother was talking about when she said, *"Leave him to heaven."* Walter was abandoned by his mother when he was eight. She left one day to go to the store and never returned. He and his brother, Darnell, practically raised themselves. He never went beyond the third or fourth grade and could barely read and write. As a child, he never had a real loving family, only the care of his grandmother. He learned life by traveling down its hard, punishing roads that showed no compassion, forgiveness, or kindness. In the end, he was giving back to his family the experiences he was given. Hurt people, hurt people.

Shortly before his death, I was visiting my mother, who, herself, was ailing with cancer, and he also was critically ill with cancer. In fact, he was in his final days. I remember him sitting on the couch looking at me with a deep, strange, almost terrified expression. His eyes were bigger than usual because of his extreme weight loss, and they were tearful. He looked at me and asked if I loved him. I looked at him and said with sincerity that I loved him. He said he was sorry for all the things he had done. I told him they happened a long time ago and I had no ill feelings towards him. That night, he had a medical crisis, and we rushed him to the hospital. I had to return to New York the next day. Walter died a few days later. I preached his eulogy the following week. While he had accepted Jesus Christ as his personal Lord and Savior when he was a young man, he never understood the Cross's forgiving grace, and he never could forgive his mother or himself. Of course, I didn't know his final thoughts, but I hope he came to understand the love of Jesus and the love of his family. He never knew the love of his own mother, and that left an indelible scar on his soul.

Over the years, this *"leave it to heaven"* advice has served me well. I've used it myself in various counseling sessions. **Revenge and the absence of forgiveness are terrible burdens to carry.** The most damaging thing it does to the one who cannot forgive is that it takes away one's joy and zest for life. That's why I refuse to let myself not forgive. I am quick to let things go…let go of the pain, the hurt, and the loss.

Chapter 4

YOU'RE GOING PLACES, BE READY

When I left for college at eighteen, I didn't think about the distant future like so many of us. I knew I had been called to be a pastor/preacher, and I knew I wanted to be a college professor one day, but I didn't have a long-term strategy. I had a little money in my pocket that I had saved while working at Safeway, and I knew I would be living on campus. I had no idea about the many unexpected opportunities that would come knocking at my door.

Subliminally, I knew I had to be ready morally, spiritually, academically, intellectually, and physically. I knew how to live in the path of blessings. The old boy scout motto comes to my mind: *Be prepared.* And it further states that we are to be physically strong, mentally awake, and morally straight.

Blessings aren't found everywhere. They are found mostly in the places God said he would bless—that is, in following the principles of God's word.

Submission is the path of blessings. I somehow always knew I was protected and I'd somehow graduate from college and go to graduate school. In the middle of my freshman year, my money ran completely out. I was broke without a penny to my name and couldn't expect to receive any money from home. Here I was, living in Texas, 600 miles away from home, with no money. I'd sometimes hear about how my fellow students would get mail from home laden with a few bucks to keep them going. I got mail from my mother, but seldom any money. She gave me something more valuable, encouragement and her prayers. She was constantly telling me that God had a wonderful plan for me. This was vague, but it gave me, oddly enough, a sense of calm. I never once complained. The dorm gave me shelter and I had food in the cafeteria. That was enough. While I am basically an introvert, I am quick to engage in conversation with anyone at almost any time. I enjoy solitude with my thoughts. My fellow students, whom I came to spend time with, were good companions. We'd share stories about our backgrounds. I thought many of them also came from humble means, but we were now all sharing a similar educational experience.

To this day, I support Historically Black Colleges & Universities (HBCUs). These institutions are the single most valuable conduit through which many black people can obtain a college education. Many successful black professionals began their college careers at an HBCU. Many years later, I met Mrs. Betty Obiajulu. She was the Long Island chairperson for the annual HBCU fundraising campaign, and she asked me to be the chairperson for black churches. We did quite well over the years. With pride, I can say that Memorial Presbyterian Church raised the most money among all the black churches.

I spent part of a semester at Linfield College in McMinnville, Oregon, as part of a cultural exchange program. The student body was 99% white. Many of them had never even talked to a black person. I was out of my element, but I had a fantastic time there. However, I shall never forget my first night in the dorm, having a conversation with my new roommate. He said, "I like you. You don't act like other colored people. You speak differently." I knew what he meant, but he didn't know that I knew what he meant. It was a harmless statement but reminded me clearly that racism and stereotyping were ubiquitous. It allowed me to educate him and other students at Linfield College. I hope I represented my race well. One must take advantage of every opportunity to tear down the walls of bias or stereotypes. I made this my mission while in Oregon.

Bishop College allowed me to develop relationships with other student preachers. We often would be invited to preach in different churches in Dallas and in other neighboring states. Once a year, about twelve of us students would organize a travel trip to Oklahoma and Louisiana. Upon arrival, we'd each be invited to preach at a different church. Every church gave each of us an honorarium as a means of helping us get through school. At the end of the day, we'd place all of our money into one pot and then subdivide the proceeds among us before driving back to Dallas. Those annual preaching forays were as useful as they were memorable. We were able to each have a couple hundred much-needed dollars. The fellowship created a bond that is treasured to this day. All of us went on to become pastors throughout the country, some to large congregations and others to smaller ones.

When I entered Bishop College as a freshman, all I had was faith in God that somehow, someway, I'd graduate; no doubt about that. As someone said, "Faith does not believe that God can do something; faith knows that he will."

* * * *

Just because something doesn't make sense to you doesn't mean it doesn't make sense at all.

Many aspects of life cannot be planned or explained in advance. There are infinite unknown variables that intrude and make planning seem irrelevant. I had a general idea of what I wanted to do with my life, but it was vague as to how events would unfold to make my dream come true. I chose to go to New York after college, and that decision alone made all the difference for the rest of my life. While my personality and character were shaped by my mother's influence, Bishop College set the foundation for my formal education beyond high school.

Later in life, when buying some land on which to build a house with my wife Evette, I asked the construction guy the most important aspect of building a sturdy enduring house that could withstand storms. I will never forget what he told me. He said the most important elements of a house are things you cannot see. He said people choose to purchase a house because it looks beautiful and might be in the right neighborhood. Buying a house based on looks alone will make for a poor choice. You can buy a million-dollar house, but the house is worthless if the plumbing doesn't work. A house has to have water and electricity but one cannot see the pipes carrying water or wiring for the electricity. But the single most important part of the house is the foundation on which everything else depends. You can't see it, but it carries the weight of the whole house, and if it crumbles or cracks, all could be lost. I've since used this illustration many times in sermons and counseling sessions.

The most valuable things in life are things that cannot be seen.

If Bishop College was the foundation for my academic preparation after high school, New York was the walls, rooms, and roof. It was like a blind man seeing for the first time. It was the peanut butter to my jelly. I absolutely loved just about everything about the city—the people, the crowds, the museums, the restaurants, the spirit, the smells, the many different cultures and languages, the different neighborhoods, the Broadway plays, the energy, the unexpectedness and spontaneity of it all.

On my very first visit to New York at nineteen to attend a week-long orientation for my upcoming trip to the Philippines, I was mesmerized by the tall buildings and the thousands of yellow cars (taxis). I felt free to explore life in different ways. I got my first alcoholic drink in New York when I was twenty-one. Times Square was like Disneyland on steroids, especially coming from a very Christian conservative college background where it was against school policy to be seen simply holding another's hand in public. That was my experience as a guy from Denver, Colorado.

God brought me to New York to attend Union Theological Seminary, and it was there that my new exposure to Christ and his teachings took on new and deeper meanings. I was fortunate to sit in all of the classes taught by Dr. James Cone, the leading Black theologian in the nation, perhaps the world. He had recently coined a term called "Black Liberation Theology," which caught many white people and, quite frankly, many non-white people, off guard. In my entire life, I never associated theology with color. Black Liberation Theology was a whole new construct, an entirely different way of looking at Jesus, God, and humanity. Of course, we studied the mainstream theologians like Paul Tillich, Karl Barth, Molton, Reinhold Neiburh, and many others, but the study of Black Liberation Theology was a game-changer. In truth, Black Liberation Theology had little to do with the actual literal color, black. It had everything to do with the human condition, the way and how

God defines and identifies his actions in the world, the way he manifests his will, his love, and his purpose. The term "black" was used as an ontological symbol pointing to the reality of those who are oppressed, who are disenfranchised, and who have been left at the bottom of the human experience. Black references the human condition of oppression and disenfranchisement. God identified with the oppressed Israelites, not the oppressor Egyptians. Jesus was born to parents of impoverished heritage. They were poor and homeless. In this sense, Jesus was black. In Black Liberation Theology, it's not what God does for the privileged class, but what God does to uplift the underclass of humanity that really matters. As Jesus said in Luke 4:18-19, His first sermon, "The spirit of the Lord is on me because he has anointed me to preach good news to the poor. He has sent me to proclaim freedom for the prisoners and recovery of sight for the blind, to release the oppressed, to proclaim the year of the Lord's favor."

Mainstream theology had endured from the very beginning of theological institutions, and it never allowed for the focus to be placed on the essence of Luke chapter 4. In fact, it permitted a perpetuation of social structures that tolerated systemic practices of racial differences, with white people always having the superior position in wealth, political power, and social authority.

White pastors graduating from these seminaries could, did, and still do serve churches that don't accept black equality. They are perfectly content in watching poor people and black people live in substandard housing, attend inadequate schools, and not have access to appropriate health services. These pastors and the congregations they serve say they are believers in Christ Jesus, yet practice a social lifestyle that is inconsistent with the Master's teaching. What's more problematic is that they can't see the incongruity of their actions compared to the scriptures' teachings. It's like the founding fathers of the United States who wrote in the constitution that stated, "We hold these truths to be self-evident that all men are created equal and endowed by their creator with certain inalienable rights and among them are life, liberty, and the pursuit of happiness." Some of the authors actually owned people as slaves. So "all" didn't pertain to black people, and it didn't include women. This myth has been promoted since the founding of this country's history. Even to this day, this dichotomy still exists.

For me, this Black Liberation Theology made all the sense in the world. I understood why my mother allowed me to drive, as a seventeen-year-old in 1964, from Denver to Atlanta, Georgia, a distance of 1,400 miles to participate in a civil rights march. When and where social, economic, and political injustice exists, one must not be silent. I had to be in a place where tangible action was being taken to destroy racism and man's inhumanity. My entire ministry has focused on helping people at the lowest rung of society, from my time working with the pimps and prostitutes in Asbury

Park, New Jersey, to the migrant workers in West Hampton, Long Island, New York, to my eager willingness to go to Memorial Presbyterian Church in Roosevelt, New York, one of the poorest villages on Long Island where I served for thirty-eight years as pastor. While the congregation grew from fewer than forty members to 1000 members, my focus was always focused on what we had to do to build up our community.

Black Liberation Theology became the backdrop for my purpose in serving God through Jesus Christ. It's why I took on the directorship of the anti-poverty agency in Roosevelt, and then the presidency of the Long Island Urban League. Our ministry developed programs for the youth of the entire community by establishing a 501(c)(3) non-profit organization, the Memorial Youth Outreach Program (MYOP), to raise money so we could reach more non-church youth. We established another 501(c)(3) non-profit organization for economic development, the Memorial Economic Development Corp. (MEDC) I served as president of both organizations.

Our most ambitious project was to work towards building a community health care facility. This vision came to me when Nassau County announced it was going to close the existing community health center for budgetary reasons. This was unthinkable in my mind. How could they do this? The Freeport/Roosevelt community health center was the only such clinic serving low-income people with no health insurance in the region for miles. The next closest one was in Elmont, many miles away, and many, if not most, of the patients didn't have personal transportation, and nearly all of them were either black or Hispanic. I petitioned the county to change its mind. I pointed out the need for such a facility. I presented charts and statistics, but to no avail.

After several meetings with the County Executive, Tom Gulotta, the County Health Commissioner, and legislators, I organized a bigger meeting with Roosevelt and Freeport residents and other clergy. After more than a year of meetings, the county finally agreed to let Memorial Presbyterian Church take the lead in an effort to try to find money to save the clinic and build another one. Our partner from the county was Hugh Mahony, Deputy Health Commissioner, truly a Godsend. I thank God for the Session (the governing elders of the local church) who trusted my leadership along with their faith in God to move forward. Over the next several years, Memorial contributed more than $200,000 to the effort. We used these funds to hire professionals when and where necessary. We had to hire architects, lawyers, proposal writers, and other consultants. After scores of meetings, and many disappointments, and broken promises, we were able to break ground for a new community health center. If we had been of weaker faith, this project would not have gone forward. I'm grateful to God for the county's eventual help in getting HUD to give us a 4.2 million-dollar grant. Tom Suozzi, the successor to Tom

Gullotta, was very helpful, finally. We are also grateful to the public county hospital for partnering with us. Without this partnership, the effort to build the clinic would have failed. In the spring of 2009, the NEW Freeport/Roosevelt Health Clinic's doors opened. The MEDC was given an office, rent-free, on the second floor as an expression of the county's gratitude for our efforts in making the new health clinic possible.

So many times over the eleven-year effort to make this happen, I was cautioned to stop, that it was not going to happen because we didn't have enough money to get the job done. But a little voice in me said to keep going. Don't stop. I think more than we realize, we miss out on blessings because we give up too soon. The MEDC board of six directors was as committed as I was, and they constantly kept saying to me, "Reggie, we can do this. We're doing to do this." Rembert Brown's voice was the most ardently consistent. He was always there urging and pushing me onward. They joined me in meeting after meeting over the years—early mornings, afternoons, and evenings. Outside of church, most people called me "Reggie" rather than Reverend Tuggle. I never minded. In fact, I welcomed it. Today, I'm told, the health clinic gets about 14,000 patient visits per year.

In its early stages, before the effort to build a community health clinic, MEDC was successful in writing grant applications to HUD for seed money. One of the major requirements of any non-profit executive is to constantly be on the hunt for funds to keep the doors open. I learned this art when working as President of the Long Island Urban League. I came to appreciate the slogan, "People don't give to causes, and they give to people."

It's not what you know or whom you know, but who knows you. I made it my business, where possible, to get to know on a personal level the personalities of those from whom I'd be requesting funds. I personally met with several chief executive officers at local banks, insurance companies, and foundations seeking money for our efforts. We met for breakfast, over lunch, or in their offices or board rooms. I was relentless. It was a tedious task and mostly unfruitful, but sometimes I was successful. As my mother would tell me, "If you don't get it, you don't get it." I am forever thankful to Robert Francis, then-Commissioner of the Town of Hempstead Commission for Economic Development, for his aid in getting us our initial funding. I learned when seeking money, one's request has to be clearly stated using the fewest possible number of words. I was told on more than one occasion that I had a strong reputation for integrity and delivering on stated outcomes.

In our early years, MEDC used the funds to purchase abandoned and boarded-up houses in Roosevelt, which were community eye-sores. They were havens for drug users, gang activity, and prostitution. We could purchase the properties for as low as $75,000 then hire local electricians, carpenters, plumbers, sheetrock contractors, roofers, and landscape personnel to do the home renovations. In effect, MEDC became a local employer. We'd place a sign on the front lawn publicizing the church's economic development initiative saying, "This home renovation project is provided by the Memorial Economic Development Corp." The members took great pride in what we were doing. The New York Times did a story on our church ministry project featuring the church and a couple of the subcontractors.

Acquiring the property was only phase two. We then had to find candidates who'd quality for purchase. HUD (Housing and Urban Development) had specific criteria. Would-be home buyers had to have an income below a certain level, no criminal record, a medium credit score, and a first-time homebuyer. But even in the effort to find qualified candidates, the church's reputation in the community for helping people find a home grew. Our office frequently got calls from people wanting to know how they could acquire a home. This is exactly what churches should be doing— helping the homeless find shelter. It was an exciting time, and all of us were proud. Phase three was to provide orientation to the new homeowners on how to get a mortgage and to show them the difference between renting and owning a home. For some people, homeownership was daunting.

God had blessed me with skills and opportunities to engage in all these things while pastoring and holding secular positions as Director of Public Affairs at Newsday for fourteen years, and later Associate Vice President at Nassau Community College (NCC) for seventeen years.

NCC is New York's largest community college with a single campus, 23,000 students (plus another 16,000 continuing education students) on 227 acres. My office oversaw all marketing initiatives, internal communications, and later, Institutional Development. The president designated me to be the Chief Information Officer. So appreciative of my time at the college, the president recommended to the Board of Trustees that I be given emeritus status, a designation reserved for only a few retiring administrators. This allowed me to retain the use of the school's email and other on-campus privileges such as library use, parking, etc., and they gave me a wonderful going away retirement party at the popular Crest Hollow Country Club. I was humbled at the extraordinary turnout from the college. Virtually every department, including the president, himself, sent representatives to see me off.

"We set the sail, God makes the wind."
—Unknown

Again, God was on the move, and by His grace, He was moving me. He knew I'd need others to travel with me to do the work that would be assigned to my hands. I had a large number of pivotal people come into my life about the time I began serving the Memorial Presbyterian Church.

Chapter 5

IT'S ALL ABOUT THE PEOPLE YOU MEET

Grace is often defined simply as unmerited favor or goodness. It's when good things happen without any particular apparent reason for goodness. Another word often used is serendipity. While I hold to that definition, I am adding something more. Grace is also the people God places in our path resulting in unexpected blessings coming to enrich our journey. Strangers we meet at a restaurant, or while sitting in a sauna, or joined on a dais at a fundraiser dinner, or casual reading of an opportunity appearing on a bulletin board, become life-altering encounters. Some of the people who crossed my path and deposited a blessing didn't always have an impressive list of credentials. They were, in nearly every instance, ordinary people with a love for God and a desire to see me go far in life.

MY BARBER

When I was eleven, I got my first job of sweeping hair off the barber's floor for two dollars a week. When I had nothing else to do and had time on my hands, I'd go and sit in Mr. Turner's barbershop. When he had no customers, we'd spend time just sitting and talking about everything and nothing at the same time. In those days, the barbershop didn't have televisions or play stations or electronic games. We had magazines and newspapers. Clients would come in and shoot the fat, talking about sports, and jive talk about what's happening in the community, women, and other stuff. Mr. Turner was an unrecognized blessing on so many levels.

He'd go with me to the school's father/son nights, he'd pay for my camp fees to attend the Boy Scout camp, Tahosa for two summers, and generally allowed me to talk to him about anything. Children need a safe place to share feelings and dreams…a place to sort things through with the ear of a caring person, a place to just be oneself. Mr. Turner was that blessing.

MOTHER PIMENTEL

Before marrying my stepfather, my mother and I would walk to church. We'd have to rely on friends, taxis, or buses to help us transport around the town. The walk wasn't long, about twenty to twenty-five minutes. We'd walk and talk to and from the church. When I got to the church, she'd go her way, and I'd join in with my friends, and we'd sit together in a separate part of the church. Sometimes, we'd sneak out to the local store and buy potato chips, sodas, Twinkies, or sunflower seeds and just play, but we'd make it back in church for the sermon.

Sundays for me were not so pleasant, generally speaking. They were very long days in the church. First, there was Sunday School at 9:30 AM - 10:30 AM, Sunday worship at 11:00 AM until about 1:30 PM or 2:00 PM, then fellowship meal after church until the 4:00 PM service, then Baptist Training Union (BTU) at 6:00 PM, and the last service at 7:30 PM until about 9:00 PM or 9:30 PM. This routine was the same almost every week. I would come home exhausted only to have to do the same thing the next Sunday.

One of the most venerated women of the Macedonia Baptist Church was Mother Pimentel. "Mother" was a title the church would confer on any woman over the age of seventy. Mother Pimentel was undoubtedly one of the oldest people on the planet. I think she was about 150 years old. I mean, she was old. She was short, stout with a large bosom, and more wrinkles than a prune.

She would always walk to church wearing the same white suit every Sunday. She was decked out with a sizeable purse over one arm to go with a large white hat with lace over her face. Her stockings were a kind of brownish/pink color and rolled up to her knees and held up with a knot on the underside to go with her white shoes. Her steps were slow with short strides. She was always alone. I learned later that her husband, a white man, had died some years earlier. She had no children.

The kids, I among them, would make fun of Mother Pimentel every Sunday. We'd laugh at her dress, her slow walk, her hat, and those crazy stockings. Every Sunday, she'd give a rather strange and unusual shout when she got happy. Often women shouted during worship service. I don't remember ever seeing a man shout. Mother Pimentel's shout was truly unique. She'd sit in the same seat, midway of the second pew. When the sermon got good to her, she'd start to rock back and forth and side to side.

And then, she'd throw her hands in the air, stand up, and give kind of a loud squeal, followed by the words, "Thank you, Jesus," and then sit down. The children would laugh and laugh and laugh. This became our weekly entertainment during the worship moment.

One Sunday, and I still can't tell you how it happened, she grabbed my arm as she was leaving the church and held me tight. The other kids laughed at me, knowing I couldn't get away. She said, "Walk me home." It was only about two blocks, and I figured I'd be back at church in no time. When we got to her house, she held onto my arm as we went inside and walked up to her apartment on the second floor. When we got to the door, I turned to leave, and she grabbed my arm again, telling me to wait until the door was opened. She reached into her ample bosom and pulled out a handkerchief with a key tied at the end. With ease, she opened the door and pulled me inside her small apartment. Then, to my young eyes, I saw with astonishment the depth and width of her world—a small cot, a small dresser, a coat rack for her clothes, one chair, and one table.

There was no TV, just a Bible on the table. I felt ashamed.

She thanked me for walking home with her, grabbed me, and pulled me close. She held me tightly, very close to her chest, and prayed. I mean, that woman prayed for me like no one had ever done. She told me God had his hand on me. When she finished praying, she let me go and said, "Go on now. Remember, I got my eye on you, boy." I felt a little weird, like something had just happened, but I couldn't identify what it was. I believe to this day, I am traveling in part on Mother Pimentel's prayers. She was an unrecognized blessing.

DEACON CLAYTON ROBB

As I mentioned, my mother was a wise woman. As a single mom, she knew I needed guidance from responsible Christian men.

At age seven, she enrolled me in the Cub Scouts, which began my seven-year stay in the scouting movement. I was always proud of the merit badges I earned for the various projects we had to complete. I began as a Cub Scout and ended as an Explorer Scout and achieved the rank of Order of the Arrow. I think just one rank lower than that of Eagle Scout, Scouting's highest honor. Deacon Clayton Robb was the Scout Leader at the Macedonia Baptist Church. I loved participating in the Scouts. He encouraged me to memorize things, the Morse code, portions of the Scouting handbook, how to tie knots, and much more. I became the scout that possessed extraordinary skills at memorizing information fast. To this day, my capacity for quick memorization has served me well. I count it as the single most important attribute to my success as a person, student, pastor, father, and manager/administrator. I remember taking chemistry in high school and was the only student in the class to memorize the periodic table flawlessly, and was singled out by the teacher for having done so.

Deacon Robb was an unrecognized blessing.

MRS. GONKEWIST

As a child, I had a speech impediment. I stuttered. I stuttered mostly when I became nervous or excited. One day, while in the eleventh grade, our speech teacher and speech therapist, Mrs. Gonkewist, said she'd work with me to overcome my stuttering problem. East High School had over three thousand students, and fewer than 100 were African American. For about six or seven months, she worked with me for one hour per day for three days a week after classes. I became so confident as a public speaker, I went on to qualify for the State semi-completion for elocution. I didn't win first place, but I did earn a ribbon and a certificate. Today, I preach every Sunday and have preached thousands of sermons over forty-six years in pastoral ministry. Hundreds of people have come to Jesus Christ after hearing the word. Mrs. Gonkewist was an unrecognized blessing. Why she came to me and offered her time and services was a mysterious act of grace.

MR. JAMES

Believe it or not, I used to be a pretty good math student. My favorite high school math teacher was Mr. James. I'm not sure how that happened, but after a while, I started visiting him almost on a daily basis for about fifteen to twenty minutes after class. We became close. I shared my emptiness with him because I didn't have a dad and I always wished to find my biological father. My stepfather and I never quite hit it off. We tolerated each other, but he drank too much, and when he did, he would become abusive to my mother and to me. I longed to find my real dad. I shared these thoughts with Mr. James and he was always encouraging, uplifting, and most importantly, forthright in urging me to not ever stop until I found my dad. I began to actively look for my biological father at eighteen and found him at age fifty-eight, forty years later. In scripture, the number forty is believed to be a symbolic number representing completion or a period of testing, trial, or probation.

> *Noah's forty days of rain*
> *The Israelites forty years in the wilderness*
> *Moses, Elijah, and Jesus fasted forty days*
> *For forty years Saul, David, and Solomon each reigned*
> *…and many more examples.*

Mr. James was an unrecognized blessing.

MR. BYERS

When I was fifteen, my mother took me to apply for a job at the Safeway grocery store, located within walking distance from our home. She encouraged me to lie about my age and say I was sixteen. It's been the only job I have ever actually applied for.

I got the job as a sacker, then later a cashier, and went for training in other aspects of running a grocery store. I was trained in produce, frozen foods, general inventory, and everything else, except for meats. Eventually, I was certified as a store manager and throughout my college days, worked summers and holidays, managing various stores for managers who took time off for vacation.

Mr. Byers was the regional manager and always looked out for me. While other students were looking for a job or work, I always had one waiting for me. All I had to do was place a call into Mr. Byers, and he'd find a place for me. I could work as many hours as I wanted. When I came home, he'd always take my mother and me out for dinner. He said I was one of the best employees Safeway had, and he wasn't about to let me go. He encouraged me to pursue a career there, but he also knew I had been called to the ministry of Jesus Christ. Altogether, I worked for seven years, summers and holidays for the grocery chain. Mr. Byers was an unrecognized blessing. I was able to pay for college in part because of my work at Safeway.

DR. JOSEPH HOWARD

When I went to Bishop College, an HBCU, I only had a few dollars in my pocket. I don't remember the exact amount, but it wasn't more than a few hundred dollars.

Like many students, I worked my way through school. I moved furniture—a job I hated, washed the cars of other students on Saturday mornings, was a clerk in the college bookstore, and did other odd jobs to keep money in my pocket. It was necessary because I only received about $100 from home across four years of undergrad. That's a total of $100 in four years, not $100 per year. During that same period, I only had one date because I didn't have money for socializing.

My sociology professor was Dr. Joseph Howard. My fellow classmates voted me as the "most studious freshman male student." My grades were generally superior to most other students. Dr. Howard and I would meet between classes to discuss social issues, religious issues, and oddly enough, my future. For some reason, he took a special interest in my future and encouraged me to apply for a junior year abroad program, which I did, the only student from Bishop to do so that year. After writing an essay and submitting my transcript, I was awarded a place in the program. I chose to go to the Central Philippine University, where at one point, Dr. Howard had taught. That year abroad was the genesis of my taking a sincere interest in international travel. Dr. Howard taught me the reason why it was important for me to embrace other cultures, languages, and traditions. He opened my eyes to my own humanity and to the wider universe. The year I spent in Asia studying Asian philosophy was one of the most pivotal years of my life. I would always see humanity as bigger and more complex than I had previously thought or known. My parochial view of life would be forever changed. Dr. Howard was an unrecognized blessing.

E. K. BAILY

God blessed me with many great friends in college, but none would leave an imprint that rivals Rev. E. K. Baily. We were roommates my senior year. I was a member of his wedding party, and he was in mine. He and I were among those students who were preparing for the preaching/pastoral ministry. We hung out together and mostly socialized among other students who were also studying for the ministry. I was a double major—philosophy and psychology. We'd practice preaching to each other in the dormitory in the evenings, and sometimes we'd go to a local diner for a hamburger or pizza.

Baily was the unofficial de facto leader of our little group. Even then, he was bigger than life at roughly six feet tall and about 250 pounds. Baily and I had a favorite thing the two of us would do. I was a running back for a short time in high school football and he was the linesman. He was a good 60-70 pounds heavier than I, so for fun, we'd line up against each other and try to knock the other down with body blows. I never won, but he knew I could hit harder. Over time, Bailey and I became really close.

We all knew God had a special call on his life and he'd become one of God's greatest servants, and he did. Wow! What a great preacher. He founded the EK Baily Institute for Expository Preaching in Dallas, Texas. I later became a Presbyterian pastor, but he and I never lost our special friendship over the years. He would later preach my late wife's (Marie) eulogy. When I called to tell him about her transition to glory, he asked when the service was going to be and told me he'd be there. He preached a powerful message. One of the most memorable statements from his sermon is:

> *"I walked a mile with Pleasure. She chatted all the way;*
> *But left me none the wiser for all she had to say.*
> *I walked a mile with Sorrow. Never a word said she;*
> *But oh, the things I learned that day,*
> *when Sorrow walked with me."*

A few years later, he would come back to Memorial Presbyterian Church to preach one of his last revivals. I could tell when he came to us that he wasn't quite himself physically. Shortly after returning to Dallas, where he pastored the Concord Baptist Church, one of the largest churches in Dallas, he called to tell me he had cancer in the sinus region of the head. We called each other often, and we'd talk and pray. Shortly before his passing, he invited me to preach at Concord. I was shocked when I saw how much weight he had lost and that he was only able to walk with the aid of a walker.

When he passed on to glory in 2003, I went down to Dallas for the funeral service. It was packed. Thousands of people from all around the country came to express love and grief for this great man of God. Rev. Baily became one of America's premier preachers and evangelists. A part of his incredible legacy is the E.K. Baily Ministers' Institute, which continues to train thousands of preachers domestically and internationally. When we were forming a lifelong friendship in college, I had no idea initially what a blessing he would be in my life.

VERNON ALLEN

In my freshman year, I was fortunate to meet and later become a mentor and friend to a great guy, Vernon Allen. Vernon suffered from one major ailment, acute asthma. So bad was his asthmatic condition, he could barely walk more than fifty yards before experiencing a need to rest. His condition was so severe that one or two days a week, he was confined to his dorm room, causing him to miss several classes. I don't think Vernon weighed more than 110 pounds soaking wet. Yet he and I would spend considerable time visiting each other and sharing life experiences. He had been sickly all of his life, and for him, a major goal was to finish college.

The summer between our freshman and sophomore year, Vernon drove up from his home in Oklahoma to spend a week with me in Denver. I was surprised he drove all the way by himself. Mother tried her best to "fatten him up," but she failed in spite of her considerable efforts. While I had to work at Safeway during the day, we spent time together after work. One of the most unforgettable things I did in my life was to drive Vernon to the Royal Gorge Bridge in Canon City, Colorado, a distance of about 125 miles. With its height at 955 feet over the Arkansas River, it is one of the world's tallest and longest suspension bridges.

Vernon was beside himself with delight. We laughed and told lame jokes and stories. He told me it was the most fun he'd had in his entire life. Just before driving back to Oklahoma, a couple of days later, we embraced, prayed, and he got in his car. Vernon died a few months after that. He was a blessing I didn't recognize. Today, I say to our Creator, thank you for Vernon. He taught me to appreciate life, no matter what. Don't complain and smile, even when you're hurting physically and emotionally.

OTHER COLLEGE FRIENDS

Of course, I had several other college friends who blessed my life. But when one is in the business of actually living each day, it's quite easy to simply think of friends as people with whom you share life without thinking that God has placed you in proximity with one another for a purpose. It's not that we take people for granted; people who would become friends, but we take them as they are without thinking anything about what they are or were meant to be. Some people become friends that enrich life in bigger ways than others. Some add richer content to life over and over again.

REMBERT BROWN

Without question, the single most important person in my life for more than forty years was Mr. Rembert Brown. He was a ruling elder at Memorial Presbyterian Church (MPC) when I arrived in 1973. He had the energy of ten people.

Rembert, a retired army veteran, was always involved in the life of the church. He had the discipline to know what had to be done and would not stop until the job was successfully accomplished. He was a bulldog. It was largely because of his assistance and foresight that I could stay at MPC for thirty-eight years. Because of his integrity as a person and his commitment to the Lord, he commanded the respect of all who knew him. When he spoke in Session meetings or before the congregation, people listened and generally did what he suggested. Everyone knew he was acting in the best interest of all and not himself. In fact, he sacrificed much personally to ensure things got done, spending his own funds and voluntarily giving of his considerable time. As president of the church's board of trustees, he was able to skillfully negotiate with banks, our neighbors when we tried to purchase their homes for necessary land acquisition to build a larger facility, and different church ministries. He and I were a team, and everyone in the church recognized our partnership. He was the father I never knew as he treated me as a son, and I loved Rembert Brown. Every pastor engaged in church growth needs a "Rembert Brown," a servant brother or sister who can be relied on in all circumstances. I can say in all candor that had it not been for Rembert Brown, the two church buildings may not have happened.

SIMON MARSHALL

By sheer numbers, the population of women outnumbers men by a large margin in most churches. Some say at least four to one, and I've seen estimates as high as ten to one or higher. Either way, the number of women in most churches far exceeds the number of men. I have said, jokingly, that there are more women in heaven than men. Hmmm. This reality held true for Memorial as well, but something happened along the way. We always had a significant men's ministry, but when Simon Marshall joined the church, he brought a new and fresh commitment to men's ministry.

I don't remember how we met, but over time we became good friends. I noticed early on his love for the work of the Lord in trying to make men into better Disciples of Christ. Later, he was elected to be president of the Men's League, and we did some remarkable new things. It was a fresh approach to reaching men and helping them grow in a stronger relationship with God. We'd have breakfast two or three times per month, and each time he was always concerned about how we could better serve the spiritual needs of men.

We had annual retreats in rustic areas of New Jersey, Pennsylvania, and upstate New York. At these retreats, we spent significant time focusing on issues that pertain to black men—health matters, relationships with wives and children, how to be a more effective spiritual leader in the home, prayer, brotherly love and support, sex, managing time, preparing for retirement, managing money, and all this with a Bible in hand for reference. We brought in guest speakers, did paintball warfare outings, river rafting, and softball games. Every Saturday morning, we had a weekly Bible study. And to no one's surprise, the number of men coming to Memorial grew and grew. Our presence in the local county jail expanded to once per month, and some of those imprisoned men, upon release, would start showing up in church on Sundays.

In 2000, Simon and I had an opportunity to go to Kenya for two weeks to study the work of the Presbyterian Church in East Africa. Today, Simon is still fostering men's growth in ministry to our Lord.

PAM ANDERSON

Sitting in the congregation as I officiated the funeral services of one of our members was Pamela Anderson. She came to me following the service dressed in dirty clothes, unkempt hair, and a significant odor about her. She was crying and told me that the person whose life we had just celebrated was her aunt. She kept saying she wanted to be a better person and asked if I'd meet with her. We set a date and a few days later, I saw her, still wearing the same clothes, hair in the same way, and the odor still present. She reached out to me and shook my hand and said she hoped I would come. She told me, so often people say they'll meet but never show up. When I arrived at the church a few days later for our 7:00 PM meeting, she was waiting.

For more than two hours, she told me her life story. In the eighth grade, she dropped out of school and became a heroin addict and crack head prostitute. She showed me the track marks on her arms and legs. She had been arrested several times and at that point had two children, one in foster care and the other in an upstate facility for juvenile boys. She had never married, and had never been baptized and knew nothing at all about Jesus. She said she was moved emotionally by the funeral service we conducted for her aunt and wanted to know more.

We met weekly for about two months. At the end of each session, I'd pray. One day she said she wanted to pray, and she did. Shortly after, she accepted Jesus Christ as her Lord and Savior, and we baptized her in a pool of a local Baptist church with several elders from MPC in attendance. Pam was a hard nut to crack. You can take the woman out of the street life, but you cannot always take the street life out of the woman. I had to help her find housing several times before we finally turned the situation around. I remember one night the phone rang at 2 AM. It was Pam again seeking help. I got up in the middle of the night to find her and placed her in a local motel for a few days. Our deacons paid her bill. My wife wanted to know, "What you and Pam got going on, here? Where are you going at two o'clock in the morning?" We got her housing, then worked to get her kids back, then a Section 8 house, then public assistance. Next thing I knew, she's volunteering her time in the local Nassau County jail talking to inmates.

Pam joined the church and started our prison ministry with such a powerful witness that many people in the congregation began working with her. One Sunday, she asked permission to speak before the congregation. She spoke for about ten minutes, telling us her story including, dropping out of school, heroin addiction, prostitution, drug use, losing custody of her two children, and homelessness. She told us Jesus had changed her life and she was never going back to her old life. She thanked the congregation for taking her in and showing love to her. The love of the congregation was more than what she ever thought possible. She became a torch for the Lord, lighting the way for others to follow her.

About two years later, I got a call in my office at the college from Pam, and she asked if I could come immediately. I did. She told me she had just found out she had AIDS and it was critical. I was with some of the church's deacons when I held her hand as she took her last breath about a year later. Standing around her bed were her two children and her other aunt. The sanctuary was packed for her funeral service with church members and people from the jail, correction officers, prostitutes, drug addicts, and members of the homeless population—all the people she had reached for the Master.

Our prison ministry became and remained a powerful witness for Christ Jesus. Shortly after Pam's death, April Cofield, another warrior with a similar history brought to the church by Pam, continued the prison ministry and made it grow. April and I worked effectively together until I retired. April wrote a book, *From Crack to Christ*, where she tells her story and the role the church played in her recovery.

THE CORE

Every pastor needs to have a core of individuals to count on no matter what the task or its difficulty. I was blessed to have about thirty such people throughout the congregation. They had my back regardless of the situation. They would be the ones to echo my vision, motivate others to participate, by leading by example, by always being present in critical meetings, giving me sage and critical advice to save me from myself, by praying for me, and helping every opportunity they got. I could write a book on the contributions of each one. When I made mistakes, and I made more than a few, they were there with relentless support and correction. I never felt abandoned by this group.

My actions and reactions at the church were focused on serving the community through the lens of scripture. The community had lots of needs, and many people needed to hear the gospel and, prayerfully, come to recognize their mortality and come to the Lord Jesus. I knew intuitively where I thought God had me headed, but the daily specifics hardly entered my awareness. All I knew was that I was quite comfortable knowing God had my back. I was responsible for the labor, handled the increase by His grace. How, when, and why God would do what God does, was His domain alone.

While I served as a pastor, I was also committed to my work at Newsday. How did the Newsday job offers happen?

God amazes me time and time again. When I was working for the Town of Hempstead, I also was the co-chair of the annual county-wide Martin Luther King, Jr. scholarship luncheon. In collaboration with the County's Office of Hunan Rights, we produced the largest and most diverse luncheons in the county. About six hundred people from different walks of life attended. Corporate donations made the scholarships possible. Newsday had become one of the corporate sponsors.

One day when I could no longer work for the Town's Presiding Supervisor for personal political reasons, Mr. Sam Ruinsky, Vice President of Community Affairs at Newsday, came to my office. He knew of my interest in fighting for civil rights. He suspected I was having a difficult time psychologically working for a guy who was running for the U.S. Senate as a conservative Republican. I told him it was hard to come to work each day. I was conflicted emotionally by working for a conservative republican who was running against Senator Jacob Javits, a progressive Republican. The candidate's platform was antithetical to what my whole life was about. Sam told me not to worry about how I was going to pay my bills if I had to leave. I'd be hearing from Newsday soon.

Sure enough, a call came in a few weeks, and I was invited to a meeting with the publisher, Mr. David Laventhol, and Don Wright, president at Newsday. After our meeting, they made a significant offer and I accepted. Sam became for me at Newsday what Rembert Brown was for me at MPC. Sam blessed me in ways I still celebrate to this day. Although Sam was a Jew, his wife and children asked that I bring the eulogy at his funeral. We had become like family. I also officiated the wedding of his son, Steve.

Every working person needs to have at least one co-worker who will become a close friend. For me, that person was Larry Levy, a talented reporter who was later promoted to the editorial board. Larry was one of those people who was wise about so many things. While he wrote mostly about politics as a political pundit and analyst, he was helpful in offering perspectives on broader life events. As our friendship developed, I came to rely on his insight for what was happening at Newsday and in my personal life. He would also confide in me.

To this day, I credit Larry with providing profoundly useful advice when my wife, Marie, died. He knew the depth of my grief and my pain. We shared many emotionally rewarding lunches and dinners. I could tell him things I didn't feel comfortable sharing with anyone else. He's also a pretty good golf buddy. Serendipity strikes again. God was looking out for me—going and coming, standing and sitting, in season and out of season, in the pastorate and in the secular arena. God's grace abounds.

Chapter 6

ACADEMIC PREPARATION

When people ask, "What school did you go to?" I say I went to three undergraduate and three graduate schools. I've earned multiple degrees in divergent fields of study. I began my college career at Bishop College in Dallas, Texas. In many ways, I suspect, Bishop was a typical HBCU where many, if not most, of these institutions' students came from humble backgrounds.

Tuition was modest as per the standards of most of the mainstream colleges, dorm life was meager, and social life was very sparse. As a religious institution, Bishop had many restrictions, most of which students observed only in public. The dorm curfew was 9 PM for freshmen, 10 PM for sophomores, 11 PM for juniors, and midnight for seniors. There was a periodic roll call to enforce these curfew rules, but mostly, they were ignored.

Male and female students were not allowed to hold hands in public. Female students had to wear skirts or dresses, with stockings or socks. Moreover, they were not even allowed to wear shoes with open toes in public. Male students had to wear shirts tucked into their pants. I remember when one of our male students, Miles Crawford, had to come before the entire student body and give a public apology for kissing his girlfriend in public to avoid suspension. His apology was embarrassing for him and for all of us, but that was the school culture at the time, 1965-69.

Because most students came from meager backgrounds, and given the dubious food quality in the cafeteria, students became very creative in supplementing our diet. We used hot plates, which was illegal, in the dorm for makeshift meals. We made sardine, spam, potted meat, and tuna sandwiches and kept our own hoard of cookies, crackers, and soda. The unspoken rule was that if one had something, we all had a right to ask for it to be shared, and usually, it was. If one didn't share, it would not be promising for his future when he needed something. His lack of sharing would be remembered. I didn't recognize it, but these tough times were, in fact, a blessing to all of us. It taught us to be resourceful without complaint.

President of Sophomore Class

At the beginning of each year, the students would be allowed to elect class presidents. In my freshman year, I was awarded the title of the "Most Studious Freshman Male" and I was elected Sophomore Class President. I didn't know how much of a blessing that would become.

Later in the school year, Dr. Martin Luther King Jr. visited our campus and gave a rousing and powerful speech. It was at a time when the nation was undergoing a critical debate about civil and human rights. It was the time of the Black Power Movement's birth, afro hairstyles, demonstrations, and protest marches.

As a member of the student council, I was invited to join with other class presidents for dinner at the home of the school's president, Dr. Milton Curry. I remember that meal so well. We all walked into the house wearing our suits, white shirts, and ties. There, in the dining room, stood Dr. King. We shook hands, made introductions, and soon were asked to come to the dinner table. The food was excellent, but the spirited discussion during and after the meal made the experience RICH. I was thinking had I not been elected class president, I would not be having dinner with Dr. King. Elected to the office of class president was an unrecognized blessing.

Other national leaders came to Bishop including Muhammad Ali, Whitney Young of the National Urban League, Vice President Hubert Humphrey, industrialists, business leaders, preachers of national acclaim, and many other powerful and rich people. The decision to begin my college career at Bishop was an unrecognized blessing. It set the stage for what was to come for the rest of my life.

The educational experience set the foundation for what was coming next. Many Bishop graduates went on to pursue graduate degrees at other mainstream schools. I was awarded a five-year PhD fellowship to study at Harvard University. They flew me to Cambridge for an interview and later made the offer. I, maybe foolishly so, declined because I wanted to live in New York. I was awarded the prestigious Rockefeller Theological Fellowship. So, I went to Union Theological Seminary with my expenses paid by the fellowship.

Going to New York was a pivotal moment in my academic life. I learned about Bishop College from my mother, who had a single conversation regarding her son's future with Rev. Joseph Griffin, our pastor at Macedonia Baptist Church.

UNION THEOLOGICAL SEMINARY

I knew I had somewhat lived a sheltered life, but didn't quite know how protected I was until I went to Manhattan. I was there to attend Union Theological Seminary, one of the nation's most renowned theological institutions. Nearly all of our professors had multiple degrees from prestigious institutions around the world like Harvard, Yale, Oxford, Cambridge, and Princeton, to name a few.

The academic rigor was more than I anticipated by far. Each professor approached his class as though his work was the only work his/her students had to master. So, each professor assigned prodigious amounts of reading material and papers to write. We had precious little time for socializing. Every night and every weekend was packed with trying to fulfill the academic requirements. It was tedious.

The primary stimulus for doing the work was the

classroom discussions, where the number of students was never more than fifteen to twenty. The last thing any student would want is to be called on and not be able to contribute. It was embarrassing to not be prepared. Many, if not most, of the Union students came from established mainstream colleges and universities. There were only a handful of African American students in the entire school and only four black faculty. The ability to express oneself verbally and in writing was measured and assessed by one's fellow students and the professor as well. The tension was generally almost always present. I loved it. I loved school, the research, the reading, the writing of papers, the classroom discussions— all of it.

Union prepared me for the next academic stop.

After graduating from Union, I was admitted to the Ph.D. program at Yale University. I owe my acceptance into Yale based on the rigorous training students experience at Union Theological Seminary and its reputation for academic excellence.

Another reason why the Union was an unrecognized blessing is because of my extracurricular experiences that would not have happened anywhere else. First, as a second-year student (seminary training is a three-year full-time program to earn a Master of Divinity degree), I was invited to serve as the Calvary Presbyterian Church pastor in Asbury

Park, New Jersey, located sixty-two miles from New York. It was a small church of about thirty members. The parsonage adjacent to the sanctuary was a frame building with no hot running water. I remember when I spent one summer there having to boil water on the stove and then take the pot of hot water on the second floor and pour it into the bathtub. By the time I got the third pot of water to the tub, the water was cold again. But that was my lot in life, and I didn't mind the inconvenience.

I was young, idealistic, and full of energy for the Lord. I was determined to preach the gospel of salvation to ALL. I would go into the local bar on Springfield Street, the main drag, with my clergy collar on and talk about Jesus. I'd go out with my portable speaker microphone and stand on a box and preach to the public walking by. My good friend, Moses Williams, would often accompany me. He'd help me set up and then help gather a crowd and shout "amen," "preach brother," and people would stand and listen. The elders of the church didn't appreciate their pastor preaching on the street corner, and they let me know about it. However, it didn't stop me.

I got to be very friendly with the local pimp. One day he came by the parsonage and sat on the porch, and we talked about his "employees" coming to church. Well, one Sunday, he and his employees came to church dressed in their uniforms: make-up, short skirts, wigs, high heels, and all. They took a seat and I welcomed them from the pulpit. The church members were not impressed. How could they come into the house of the Lord dressed like *that*? I was asked by a couple of the elders to instruct our guests that in the future, if they decide to come back, they must be dressed more appropriately. I reminded them of what the Lord said, "Come just as you are." My response didn't go over very well.

I had to get up at 5:30 AM to get dressed and take a subway to Penn Station, where I caught the Path Train to Asbury Park, then walk twenty minutes to the church—rain, snow, or sleet. I'd preach, and then with an elder driving, I'd visit the sick and return to Manhattan by six or seven that night. The church began to grow. By the time I left the church, we had embarked on a building program two years later. My successor was able to continue the work and finally built a new church. He went on and changed its name from Calvary Presbyterian Church to the Martin Luther King Presbyterian Church. The church prospered, thanks to the Holy Spirit.

Calvary was an unrecognized blessing because that is where I met Rev. Paul Sobal, the Executive Presbyter of Monmouth County, New Jersey. Rev. Sobal would later introduce me to Rev. Bill Rambo who would present me an opportunity to work with migrant farm workers. I was recommended to serve at the Calvary Church by Union's president, Dr. Lawrence Jones. He told me I was open-minded and willing enough to take on the assignment.

The second significant event happened when, during my

senior year at Union, I was elected to be the black student caucus president. It was a turbulent time in America in 1971-72. The Women's movement (N.O.W.) was just getting off the ground and there were constant and very demonstrative anti-Vietnam protests around the country.

There came a time when there was a large anti-Vietnam war protest rally at Columbia University across the street from Union. It was held in the quad, a huge space in the middle of the campus. Thousands of protestors, mostly students, gathered to hear speakers rail against the war.

One of the keynote speakers was Congressman Rev. Adam Clayton Powell, a nationally recognized civil rights leader and arguably one the most powerful black leaders in New York City. I was one of several student speakers. In my remarks, I said I could no longer in good conscience support the war in Vietnam. I could no longer sing "God bless America" when our soldiers drop napalm bombs from B52 bombers from 45,000 feet on innocent villages, killing thousands of women, men, and children. I could no longer sing" God bless America" when we were deploying the Agent Orange chemical, causing the defoliation of millions of acres of forests and polluting rivers and lakes. I said more. I would rather we sing either God Save America or God Damn America.

The next day, an article about the rally appeared in the New York Times. There was a quote from me saying that Reginald Tuggle, a Union Theological student, said God Damn America. It gave only the gist of my remarks, but it didn't give the full context to my statement. That's how it made it appear that I was saying God Damn America without mentioning what the damnation was for.

The seminary president called me into his office the next day. As I walked in, he had on his desk a copy of the New York Times. I was expecting a reprimand. None came. Instead, he held up the paper and said to me, "I see you made the paper today. Good job."

The third major event that shaped my future came about three weeks later. I got a call from Congressman Powell's office. Rev. Powell was also the renowned Abyssinian Baptist Church pastor in Harlem, which had a rich history of engaging in civil rights and economic development. I went to the interview held in the upstairs office space of the Duncan Funeral home. When I arrived, the congressman was conducting a staff meeting. I waited to stand at the door until I was recognized.

Finally, he turned to me and said, "Good speech, boy (obviously referring to the rally held a couple of weeks earlier). Do you pay your taxes, son?" He was wearing a black turtleneck and smoking a cigar. I told him I paid my taxes on time. He continued, "Ever been arrested, son?" I told him no. Apparently, he had some knowledge of my transcript.

"I see you're a pretty good student." I told him I enjoyed school and class assignments. Congressman Powell asked if I had ever been arrested and if I paid the IRS on time. Then, out of the clear blue and in the presence of everyone in the room, he said, "Would you like to work for me, boy?" I was surprised but said yes. I would be honored. He turned to his Chief of Staff, Mr. Odel Clark, and told him to make sure I got all the clearances required from Washington in order to bring me onboard.

It took several more weeks before I was assigned to work in his Harlem Office for Constituent Services. This position was an absolutely awesome job. I learned how local politics worked in Harlem, who were the HNICs in the community, and why and how things were done. John Lindsey was New York's mayor at the time. I enjoyed going to community meetings with Rev. Powell, hearing him speak with such eloquence and charisma. That summer, I had a chance to study at the University of Ghana, and I opted for economics and political science. When I told Congressman Powell about the opportunity, he paid for all of my expenses. God had opened another door. My mother was right. God had great plans for me, and they were just beginning to arrive.

Chapter 7

PREPARATION BASED ON CHOICES

Upon graduating from Union in 1972, I was admitted into Yale University's PhD program. My goal was to graduate by the end of the fourth year then seek work in a situation where I could teach at a college and pastor a local church. I loved Yale. It had a different atmosphere than in New York and at Union. The city of New Haven was nothing like Manhattan. It was a college town, but it was a city of two tales with a strong middle class dominated by the university on the one hand, and on the other a struggling black community which was at best, the lower middle class.

Yale was even more demanding academically and intellectually. My fellow PhD students were friendly enough out of class, but they were very guarded about sharing information about what they were working on. Even though I looked forward to our class discussions but they were intimidating. It involved matching wits, like who would say the more insightful thought or put forth an analytical observation.

I came to look forward to the in-class discussions, but I knew I had to be prepared. The teaching style of most of my professors was to have a discussion by calling randomly on students to participate. The most embarrassing thing one could experience was to be called on and not have any thought-provoking thing to say. As the only black student in most of my classes, I felt this pressure very acutely.

I was one of the only two black students in my program, which was a hybrid between the School of Religion and the School of Business. My focus was on business ethics. I was looking at the ethical implications of multinational corporate investments in third world countries. By then, I had traveled to Asia, Africa, and Europe, so I had some limited familiarity with international culture. I had a great doctoral advisor, Dr. Chuck Powers, a renowned expert on the subject of corporate social responsibility. He was in high demand, often flying off to lead corporate discussions and retreats on the topic or serving as a consultant. Chuck, as he insisted that I call him, and I became the closest of friends. I ate at his home often, and he was gracious in sharing his spare time with me as he helped me shape my future.

In those days, the structure for completing the requirements of the Ph.D. was to do two years of in-class course work, a year of research, and the fourth year was writing the dissertation. The grading system was a little strange. Assuming one took a minimum of four courses per semester that would mean a total of at least eight courses per year or sixteen in two years. The actual grades were Honors (H), High Pass (HP), and Pass (P). Every Ph.D. student had to have at least two H grades per semester and no Ps. At the end of two years, one had to have at least eight Hs and no Ps.

Failing to meet these academic requisites would result in one being asked to withdraw from the program. I met all of the academic requirements, except the language prerequisite.

I would have to pass a GRE (Graduate Record Exam) foreign language in German, French, Italian, Japanese, Chinese, or another preapproved language by the end of the second year. I failed the GRE in German twice. I had only one more chance. So, I took the summer off and immersed myself in the study of French, ten hours a day, six days a week, for ten weeks. I passed the language requirement in French. Had I failed, I would have been disqualified for continuing into the third year. By the grace of God, I was able to remember large quantities of material. I must confess, however, I don't speak French even though I passed the test. In those days, however, I could read almost any novel or book in French and respond accurately to most questions on the GRE.

I would have completed the dissertation, but calamity came knocking at my door. I experienced a severe personal problem that had such a powerful negative effect on me emotionally, I couldn't focus on the mental rigor necessary for conducting proper research. To compound matters, I was teaching a political science course at the University of New Haven to make ends meet, and I was serving as pastor at the Community Baptist Church. I was stretched so thin I couldn't see straight. It wasn't my employment duties that caused me stress, I rationalized, it was something else that was so painful emotionally that to this day, I don't talk about it. I was disappointed in myself and in life. My relationship with scripture was non-existent, and my prayer life was weak. It was during this time that I was carried on the wings of God. I set sail, and God made the wind.

Chapter 8

WORKING WITH MIGRANT WORKERS

When my time at Calvary Presbyterian Church ended, Rev. Paul Sobal recommended Rev. Bill Rambo, the executive presbyter for Long Island. Rev. Rambo presented me with an opportunity that I would have never imagined that later turned out to be the singular most transformative experience in my life.

My first assignment in this new presbytery was to work with migrant farmworkers on Long Island's east end. Because of the wealth found in adjacent South Hampton, I was asked to work with the poorest of the poor in West Hampton, which I did for the summer of 1972. I worked with migrant potato farmers. Large and small potato farms dotted the landscape. The one thing that most of them had in common was the customary practice of hiring migrants to work on the land. Those men, along with some women and children, were mostly black. They followed the migrant farm circuit of working farms in the south during the winter and New York during the summer. They picked oranges, strawberries, other produce, and whatever they could find in the south before moving north. Many had been doing this kind of work for years. However, the living conditions were atrocious.

I had never met a migrant worker who owned a car. Most workers lived in barracks stocked with upper/lower bunk beds. They were separated; men in one barrack and women and children in the other. They worked in the fields for many hours, digging up potatoes, then washing them down for processing. Most were uneducated and/or had different underlying psycho-social issues such as alcoholism, hot tempers, and depression. Most were from the south, where a few of them had families to whom they'd send money for support. Needless to say, the pay wasn't a real living wage. Even with that, the crew chief, a man hired by the farmer to oversee the laborers, would charge them for the use of blankets, food, wine, soda, and other items. On payday, the workers were paid in cash minus their costs for blankets, food, wine, soda, etc. Payday disputes were very common, but the crew chief was there to make sure things didn't get out of hand. Armed with a gun and accompanied by two assistants who were armed with bats, he'd issue the wages and literally dare anyone to challenge his figures. It was an awful scene—painful to watch.

My task was to work with these men and convince them to leave the farm and work with a construction company established to build modular homes. We were financed by the generosity of successful white businessmen and the Long Island Presbytery. We trained the migrants in various skills required to build a house, boarded and fed them, and paid them much more than they were making on the farm. The men were very reluctant to leave a job they knew so well for a job that required them to acquire new skills for the tasks they knew nothing about. Most of the workers were fearful, suspicious of me, our organization, and what really could happen to them. I was the principal motivational teacher and tasked with the responsibility of convincing them to take the leap for a new and better life for themselves.

Every night, we'd sneak onto the farms and take as many as we could get into our cars. Then, we took them to the very private re-education site. Mr. Van Dyke Johnson, a very militant black radical, was the executive director. I reported directly to him, and we made a great team. One night, an armed crew chief came looking for me. He wanted to teach me a lesson about taking men from his farm and "messing up their minds." I was secretly sent away to a white man's home, Mr. Ed Geyer, for a couple of days until things calmed down.

Ed enjoyed playing chess, and so did I. After dinner, we'd play chess for hours and talk about philosophical constructs. To some extent, Van and I, along with our team, were successful. The construction company we worked for built about a dozen modular homes and altogether hired about fifteen men over a two-year period. This was an unrecognized blessing because it exposed me to a lifestyle and people I would have never met. But more so, it taught me humility. By that time, I already had two degrees, a certificate in economic studies from the University of Ghana, and was enrolled in graduate studies at Yale. My life was moving in a positive direction. Those men who worked at the farm had little chance of moving, probably no farther than to the next farm. I was keenly cognizant of our differences, except for the grace of God, go I. Thank God most, if not all, of the potato farms are now gone.

Chapter 9

A LIFETIME JOURNEY SERVING THE CALL

I n my mind, the pastor has a job description with only three primary requirements. First, the pastor must love the people. Second, the pastor must love the people. Third but not least, the pastor must love the people. It's the answer to the question that Jesus asked of Peter three times, "Do you love me?' There are many secondary aspects to the job description that pastors must attend to, but none will surpass these three.

Being a pastor is a calling, not a job. It's the love of the people as lead by the Holy Spirit that will compel the pastor to be available to the members and their circumstance whenever and wherever required—any time of day or night. What parishioners see us doing on Sunday morning is only a fraction of what we do throughout the week. Usually, the service a pastor gives is appreciated, but often it is a lonely job going from crisis to crisis, meeting to meeting, counseling session to counseling session, and occasionally officiating weddings. Preparing practical and inspirational sermons is quintessential to feeding the peoples' spiritual needs. Most pastors spend considerable time alone. There have been many articles about pastors experiencing depression.

It's a role where many church members regard themselves as your boss, or if not that, a member whose voice and opinion should be taken more seriously than another member. The role requires a pastor to be a negotiator, a peacemaker, and a cheerleader. He/she must successfully navigate the different cliques and factions within the congregation.

If done correctly, the role of the pastor requires him/her to put other's needs above and beyond their own. As a result of loving the people, pastors place themselves and sometimes their families at risk. I was protected from domestic family strife and excessive drama by having a sensitive and caring wife and obedient and loving children. Thank you, Holy Spirit. I often was absent from home. Fortunately, my children were well disciplined and embraced the habit of studying, even if their mother or I wasn't around to supervise.

More than a couple of times, I went into my personal savings to loan money to parishioners to help them save their homes from foreclosure or respond to other financial needs. Most of the time, I was repaid, but on a couple of occasions, I wasn't. Once the financial loss was considerable. Even so, pastors don't give up on people. When people promise to do something in the church or for the church, and they fail to follow through, pastors keep faith in them and trust in God's Holy Spirit anyway.

By far, the rewards of pastoring outweigh the

disappointments such as when a marriage is made stronger because of a ministry within the church, or when a newly released person from jail turns their life around, or when people keep joining the body of Christ and our membership numbers increase, or one shares in the successful capital campaign for building a new church, or a potential school dropout graduates from high school, or when celebrating the love between two people and then officiate their wedding and then see them become active in the life of the congregation, to see a person transition from this life to the next with a sense of joyful anticipation, or to help prepare and train people to be effective disciples of Christ and not be merely church members, or witness elders wanting to give more to the ministry by teaching Bible classes or mentor youth, or see youth enthusiastically bring their friends to church and to Bible study groups, to experience the creation of new and innovative ways to respond to the needs of the community and much more. I was blessed to have performed scores of baptisms and hundreds of weddings over thirty years, and some in destination locations like Canada, Jamaica, and The Bahamas.

With rare exception, pastoring is a job, at least in most small Presbyterian churches, that pays minimally, resulting in most pastors having to struggle financially. That's the main reason why I was always bi-vocational, holding a secular position to support me and provide for my children and their college education. The apostle Paul was a tent maker and a preacher, too. It was exhausting physically at times, but it was worth it. Sometimes when I go to a new doctor and have the pre-patient interview, I'm asked if I have any allergies. I tell them, "Yes," and they look up with curiosity and ask, "What are you allergic to?" I smile and say, "Poverty."

In May of 1973, I was called to preach at the Memorial Presbyterian Church in Roosevelt, New York, a small church that our denomination had voted to close because it had too few members and no money. None.

To justify their decision, the local judicatory voted to shut off any financial assistance in the hope that the congregants would see reality and voluntarily move their membership to other nearby Presbyterian churches. In 1992, Hollywood produced a movie entitled *A Few Good Men*, which celebrated the honor and courage of those who serve as soldiers in the U.S. Marine Corp. Well, the members who remained in the church at MPC were a few good people, full of faith and committed to making the church survive.

Since its founding in 1920, Memorial was a mission church, meaning that part of its budget was subsidized by the local judicatory, the Presbytery of Long Island. My immediate predecessor was the first black pastor, and he had his salary subsidized by the denomination. When I came on board, all financial help had dried up. Neither I nor the church got any financial assistance from external sources.

I would typically drive from New Haven, Connecticut, on a Saturday morning, visit the sick and attend community meetings. I'd preach on Sundays then drive back to New Haven Sunday afternoons, a distance of ninety-five miles, and took about one-and-half hours.

I was paid $50 a week salary plus another $15 for gas and tolls. The church was so broke that when I got the weekly check from Mrs. Freddie Ashby, I'd hear the same admonition, "Rev. Tuggle, don't cash this check 'til Wednesday." Memorial was so poor it could not cash a $65 check on a Monday. I was the only black Presbyterian pastor on Long Island at the time and remained so until Memorial called its first Associate Pastor during my twenty-fifth year as pastor. The church called Rev. Yvonne Collie Pendleton and later, Rev. Richard Crayton to serve as part-time associate pastor later.

Early on, white pastors would tell me the situation at Memorial was a lost cause and I should do the church a favor and help the members understand that it had no future. They felt sorry for me. What they couldn't understand was that even at $65 per week, this was a good situation for me. I was a graduate student, always broke, and determined to make the best of it. At the time, I was an ordained Baptist preacher, and I saw this as a temporary assignment at best. My plan was to stay two years, finish my doctorate, and move on to greener pastures as a college professor and a pastor somewhere else. In fact, I announced to the congregation that my stay with them would not be more than two years.

I was twenty-six years old and could not see myself in the situation for a long time. The church was old, dilapidated, with a leaking roof, no carpet in the sanctuary, and broken shingles. It needed painting everywhere. I remember during the coffee hour after service one Sunday, Mrs. Nina Collins partially fell through the floor in the basement because it had been weakened by termites.

But the Holy Spirit had other designs on my life.

As it would turn out, I'd stay at Memorial Presbyterian Church for thirty-eight years before my tenure ended. During that time, we grew from just under forty members to nearly 1000. By the end of my time at MPC, our church, which was unarguably the poorest in the presbytery, became one of its most powerful congregations in the region. Our total mission giving went from $500 in 1973 to more than $130,000 in 2010, including scholarship gifts, local mission, unified mission, deacons and more.

Pastors kept asking me how I turned the situation around at MPC. I always gave the same answer. I didn't do it. It was the work of the Holy Spirit. I also told them it takes some risk and a lot of hard work to move the needle forward.

You can't go forward if you're constantly looking back.

My start at MPC was less than favorable in other respects, but I didn't mind. I lived alone in the church's manse (parsonage). For eighteen months, I slept on the floor. I had hardly any furniture, except a mattress on the bare floor, one chair, a small black/white television, and that's it. I ate most of my meals at local diners as I never cooked at home, and really welcomed the opportunity to share a meal at the home of a member.

One day Elder Rembert Brown came by to visit me. He was surprised to find the house completely empty of furniture. He asked, "Reggie, where is your furniture?" I told him about my situation and took him upstairs to see the bedroom. He felt so bad and said he was embarrassed. I had lived there for a year and a half, and no elder had ever thought about my living situation. No one had ever visited me. He went out that afternoon to a local thrift furniture shop and got me a frame and box springs to place my mattress on, a two-seater couch, a table and two chairs, and a lamp for the living room. I didn't mind sleeping on the floor, but it certainly felt better to sleep with my mattress resting on box springs.

The elders wanted me to become their pastor, but I was a Baptist, and in order for me to pastor the church, I had to go through all the requirements to become an ordained Presbyterian pastor. I had the academic requirements, but I lacked Presbyterian polity. It was a lot of reading, learning Presbyterianism, and then passing an oral examination. It's not unusual for a candidate to take these exams several times before passing. I was fortunate to pass on my first attempt. So, in March 1975, a year and a half later, I was ordained a second time, but now as a Presbyterian.

I remember calling my mother and telling her of my decision to become a presbyterian. Her reaction was predictable.

"What's a Presbyterian?" she asked. "Do they believe that Jesus Christ is the only savior of the world?"

I told her that they were Christian and they believed basically as Baptists believed but their way of governance was different.

"Well, if they believe in Jesus, and if you've prayed about it and feel comfortable with it, then it's okay with me."

GROW WHERE YOU'RE PLANTED

Most black Christians are predominately in one of three denominations: Baptists, Pentecosts (holiness), or African Methodists Episcopal (AME). Most of our historical roots in Christendom is in one of these mainline traditions.

As a denomination, the Presbyterian Church (PCUSA) is part of the reformed tradition and has fewer than two million adherents. The founder of Presbyterianism was John Knox in Geneva, Switzerland, in the mid-1500s.

Today, less than 3% of the Presbyterian denomination is African American. So, growing a local congregation in a majority-black community is particularly challenging because it is not representative of the norm in expressing one's Christian perspective.

Needless to say, most of the people who joined the MPC

did not come from the Presbyterian tradition. New members came from one of the above-mentioned denominations, or they were not baptized at all. MPC did attract a few Catholics, however. Further, as our prison ministry grew, new members came to us when they were released from jail. It was an uphill battle, having to constantly explain to people who we were and what we represented. In truth, I am not a strict Presbyterian or any other denominationalist. I don't really believe in denominations. While I am pleased to serve God in the Presbyterian tradition, denominations are a man-made contrivance created for the practical establishment of institutionalized religion based on doctrinal interpretations. God doesn't live in buildings and is not confined to any church doctrine or dogma. God is God, and Jesus Is Jesus.

Only Jesus can atone for our sin, not a denomination or a dogmatic formula. My spiritual roots are anchored in Jesus alone, so with that in mind, for me to switch from being a Baptist to become a Presbyterian was a simple and painless matter. My religion didn't change, just the man-made institution where I worship the Lord on a Sunday morning. My love for the church and for what the church is supposed to do didn't change, just my outlook and my mission had expanded to be more inclusive of others. Given the remarkable growth at MPC, it would seem as though God guided me from birth for this very purpose. I was called to take on an assignment that no one else wanted, and just about everyone thought to be hopeless.

Since I had no other African American Pastors to affiliate with or to socialize with within the Presbyterian Church, I found myself always in the company of pastors who were Baptist, Pentecostal, or AME. My social and ecumenical ministry always involved these religious leaders.

When MPC had fellowship with other churches, it seldom was with a sister Presbyterian Church. We went to Baptist, Pentecostal, or AME churches for afternoon worship moments. When we went to challenge local government officials about the needs of our community, it was with all of us joining our different voices as one unified expression. What we shared were the common needs of the African American community, our disenfranchisement, and our aspirations. Our collective voice was an expression of the community's frustration of how the local government was neglecting us, our schools, our neighborhoods, and our youth.

Statistically, black youth unemployment was literally twice that of white youth. Because we made demands, for two consecutive summers, the Town of Hempstead gave every black child between the ages of fifteen and sixteen a job if they could prove their parent's income was at or below a certain level. These minimum paying jobs such as picking up trash at parks and beaches, recreation assistants, poolside assistants, and the like were welcomed.

Our congregations took great pride in their pastors fighting for their children. As pastors, we NEVER spoke from the perspective of our denominations. That reality was totally irrelevant.

Rev. Arthur Mackey, pastor at the Mt. Siani Baptist Church I Roosevelt and Bishop Ronald Carter, pastor at the Refuge Apostolic Church in Freeport, often were the lead speakers. Rev. Mackey was tall with a booming voice. Once when we had failed after many meetings with elected officials to get more black police on the County's force, he stood and said in a loud voice, "If Nassau County doesn't hire more black officers we're going to wrap this place in black." The following week all the pastors and many of our members, several hundred in all, marched around city hall. Eventually, more black police officers were hired.

Black pastors are the de facto leaders advocating on behalf of issues within the black community. For five years I served as the President of the Nassau County Council of Black Clergy. We'd talk about a wide range of issues: access to health care, high youth unemployment, police brutality, not having enough black police on the county's police force, not having enough black county and town appointments, the neglect of repairing our streets filled with potholes, etc.

We also went to political party headquarters and spoke to the respective republican and democratic chairpersons and demanded that they run more African American candidates. We wanted more black judges, more correction officers in the jail, more social workers, more town departments and county heads for black people.

These were common themes at our meetings, which usually were cordial but sometimes resulted in the raising of voices and hitting tabletops for emphasis. Sometimes to our surprise, we got what we asked for. When we didn't, we'd plan another meeting until something changed. I would report back to the congregation on Sunday mornings of our meetings with local politicians. They loved hearing about our successes and our failures.

Sometimes people characterized me as a politician. I wasn't, of course, but I was vocal in speaking out for issues I knew were critical to the health and safety of our community. Sometimes what we did caught the attention of Newsday, our local daily newspaper and I was often quoted along with others. Eventually, people started coming to MPC to hear me. The NAACP made MPC the venue for their monthly meetings. Political candidates made it a point of stopping by MPC to join in Sunday morning service and to seek my endorsement. I never endorsed a candidate from the pulpit, but if asked away from the pulpit, I always told people whom I would vote for and why.

TWO ARE BETTER THAN ONE

Working two full-time jobs wasn't always a smooth process. I had to be careful not to shortchange either. When I was at the college, for example, I never spoke about church business. When I was at the church, I rarely spoke about my job at the college except as it had a bearing on what the church was doing or had an interest in.

Newsday, as a daily newspaper, is a deadline business. The deadline impacted everything. Getting assignments in on time was critical. I am humbled to say that in fourteen years as Director of Public Affairs, I never once was late in giving my reports or completing projects. That sometimes meant I had to get up at 2:00 AM or go into the office on a Sunday afternoon or evening, but I was never late. I also made sure the three managers who reported to me were not late. Before I accepted any secular position, I made it clear that I was a pastor and that at times it may be imperative to leave my desk to attend to urgent church business. My time away from my desk wouldn't be abused, so when I left the office, it would be because of a necessity. They all understood, and I never abused this covenant.

The elders and members began to expect me to be out serving the community, and I was content to do so. With all of my secular employment positions, I asked them to permit me to participate in community events as long as it didn't interfere with my job. They agreed.

I often had to take time away from my various secular positions during the day at the Urban League as its President, or my time in the office as chief of staff to Al D'Mato, Presiding Town Supervisor, or leave my desk as Director of Public Affairs at Newsday, take time away as Associate Vice President at Nassau Community College, to conduct a funeral service, or visit someone in the intensive care unit, or attend a critical political meeting. Because I had the equivalent of two full-time jobs, my free time was very limited. I was working seven days a week and trying to raise two daughters as a single parent. (More about this later.)

My time in the community was such that by the end of my tenure on Long Island, I was blessed to have been honored by scores of organizations and Hofstra University. I received more than 300 awards and plaques for community service and service to the congregation over a thirty-eight year span. In 2010, I became the first African American to be inducted into the Queens County Asian American Hall of Fame because of the twenty-one years I had coordinated social events that brought Asian Americans and African Americans together to discuss and share common issues.

When I retired from pastoring the Memorial Presbyterian Church, the Town of Hempstead voted to name the street adjacent to the church the "Rev. Reginald Tuggle Avenue." A crowd gathered on a Saturday morning, joined by elected officials for the street sign unveiling. I have a replica of the street sign in my office, reminding me of how blessed I am by God's grace. I was, and I remain humbled by this recognition.

Chapter 10

HOW & WHY A CHURCH GROWS?

*Imagination Makes It Possible, Commitment
Assures Success*

The central motivating factor for writing this book is in response to the question: "How did Memorial Presbyterian Church grow so fast when other church situations were declining in membership, funding, and mission?" There are no simple answers, and each congregation and community is different.

Central to the congregation's thinking was our official mantra, "Imagination Makes It Possible, Commitment Assures Success." Still, I contend that there are some essential things any church must do in order for the church to grow. Effective leadership is critical in all aspects of growth, and the ministry of the congregation must respond to the spiritual, emotional, and material needs of the members and the community. What follows are the many things that happened to cause growth to occur at MPC. It's a remarkable story which once heard, will inspire others.

As MPC began to experience rapid growth, I was often asked to speak at conferences and seminars across the country. Staff at the General Assembly would invite me to share our story with small churches and tent-making conferences. Tentmaking is the term to reference preachers in our denomination who worked secular jobs in addition to pastoring. After several years of accepting these invitations, I was asked at a conference in Albuquerque, New Mexico, by a group of pastors, "How does it feel to pastor the same church for 25 years?" I told them, "I don't know. It's not the same church and I'm not the same pastor." Then I'd say in all seriousness that the growth at MPC had happened because of hard work by the church members and the leadership of the Holy Spirit.

By that time, MPC had become the largest black Presbyterian Church in the State of New York. As I mentioned earlier, most black people are not Presbyterian, so growth of any kind was considered remarkable.

After finishing my in-class course work requirements at Yale, it allowed me to live in Roosevelt full-time. I asked the Elders permission to work a secular job with the pledge not to neglect my pastoral responsibilities. I'd be available for counseling, hospital and sick visits, and preaching. They agreed. The Presbytery of Long Island strongly objected, however, saying my role was to serve the church and the church only. They didn't like for their pastors to work outside the bounds of a pastor. Their unexpected reaction was the first of future non-supportive responses that soured my taste in working with the local judicatory. I couldn't understand it because they knew my income from the church was insufficient to live on, and I felt it wasn't their business to weigh in on what the local elders and the congregation had agreed to do. I got no support from fellow white pastors. In fact, one pastor told me directly that my taking on a secular job was totally unacceptable. I thought at the time that it was because I was the only black pastor.

I felt alone and abandoned by the group that had enthusiastically ordained me to serve only a few months earlier.

Without support or endorsement from the Presbytery, I took on the job of executive director of the Roosevelt Anti-Poverty Agency (the Roosevelt Economic Opportunity Commission) In my interview with Mr. John Kearse, the Executive Director of the Nassau County Economic Development Corp., I was a little nervous. John Kearse was a very tall, broad-shoulder black man with a goatee, deep-set eyes, and a huge afro. He had the reputation as a bigger-than-life warrior, fighting for poor people and civil rights. He spoke with a slow, clear, and precise cadence. Nearly everybody felt intimidated in his presence. The EOC operated eleven anti-poverty agencies throughout Nassau County, all in low-income areas. Nassau County was one of the wealthiest counties in America, yet it had these pockets of vast economic disparity.

I will never forget sitting in John's office and having to respond to his first question. Taking a cigarette, he leaned back in his chair, took a draw and said, "Reggie Tuggle. Reggie Tuggle. Why are you, a grad student at Yale

University, interested in working in an anti-poverty agency?" Then before I could respond, he continued, "What do you think you can bring to an agency that helps poor people?" Great questions. That gave me a chance to share my life story, my values, my approach to life, my commitment to help and serve others. We talked for nearly four hours. I was surprised how fast time seemed to have gone. I worked with the EOC for a year and a half before I was asked to become the president of the Urban League of Long Island. During my time with John, I learned so much about how to forge ahead as a black leader in the face of abuses from white people and quite often from black people.

My early years at MPC were productive, even though at the time, I didn't have a well-articulated strategic plan. My first thought was to build a youth ministry.

We had about a dozen youths in the church. I often spent my Saturdays out at the local basketball court. I'd hang out on the side of the court, and when the players came to the side between games, I'd have a brief conversation with them.

"Hey, you're pretty good out there. My name is Reverend Reggie Tuggle, and I pastor the Memorial Presbyterian Church down the street."

Then they'd say something like, "Yeah, I know the church." Or "No, never heard of it." Or "No, I never went to the church." Or "No, I don't go to church."

Then I'd give them my prepared speech about me trying to build a youth ministry, about having a free pizza party at the church next Friday night at 6 PM and they were invited and to please bring a friend if they'd like. I did this for many Saturdays. I became a fixture at the court. After a while, I'd walk in the gated court and be welcomed with shouts of "Hey, Rev. Tuggle, how you doin'?" and "'I'll be at church next Friday. Have the pizza ready."

First only one or two came, then more and more. Before long, they were coming to church on Sunday morning, and then later with their parents. If a church can attract youth, youth will bring parents. It works almost every time.

Although I began as the youth minister, I quickly had help from the older MPC youth, Monique Reid, Denise Wallace, Joy Williams, Jill Williams, Natalie Bethea, Ian Francis, Lionel Lyons, Donna McLaren, and Pattie Williams. We'd go skating, to plays, play sandlot sporting events, and enjoy basketball, softball, field days with track events, three-legged races, picnics, and more. We always had some sort of Bible study.

Some even joined the effort to start a youth choir. For several years the MPC youth organized a village-wide field day where ten to twelve churches joined in with us by sending their youth to the event. We'd have events at the high school track then all of us would go over to the nearby park for a picnic after handing out ribbons. There were no winners or losers. Each participating church provided food and drinks.

It was a wonderful day of community unity and sharing

the spirit of Christ working with and among all of us irrespective of church affiliation.

God has a way of doing things that, when they are done, all one can do is scratch your head. When I was coming down from New Haven for a weekend, I'd spend time on Saturday nights meeting with local community leaders. I wanted to know what the five most critical issues in Roosevelt were. We met for several months, debating and analyzing the community. They identified the following issues as being critical: inadequate public education, teenage pregnancy, high school dropout rates, the lack of public service response to things like garbage pick-up, the lack of curbs on some streets, thus causing flooding in certain parts of the village. My initial goal was to have the church host as many community meetings as possible. I wanted the church to be the venue that people looked to for meaningful social action.

Up until this point, MPC was never regarded as a viable community ministry. That was not my predecessor's forte. **In this regard, the community leaders, at my suggestion, sponsored a series of community forums on critical issues.** Our first meeting was held in the basement of the church on the topic Taxation Without Representation. We passed out flyers, made phone calls, got pledges from community organizations to attend. The County Executive, Mr. Ralph Caso, came with his deputies. It was a great meeting. It was the first time for many Roosevelt citizens to ever have the opportunity to have a face-to-face discussion with the highest elected official in the county. After making the opening statement of purpose, I turned the meeting over to one of their trusted leaders to continue with the agenda. From that one meeting alone, we got new curbs installed a few months later on the streets needing them. The people felt empowered and encouraged, and MPC was on the map.

The second forum focusing on teenage pregnancy was also held in the church. We invited social workers, school officials, doctors, and parents to be panelists. It was a more descriptive discussion and very light on prescriptions. It takes a village to raise a child, and everyone felt some level of responsibility for this tragic phenomenon. We all accepted some measure of shame and blame. It was more cathartic than helpful, but it was a useful event in that we all saw ourselves as a community trying to deal with a very difficult problem.

Our third forum was on why there was such a high percentage of Roosevelt residents living on social welfare. Why wasn't the public assistance load shared throughout the county? We all knew the reason, but we wanted to hear county officials admit to it. They had created a ghetto by design with the aid of realtors and the social services department, and we were bearing the brunt of it.

The Roosevelt village was a great example of how race manifests itself in public policy.

Until 1969, Roosevelt was majority white. Then there was an extraordinary shift in racial demographics. By 1975 the majority of the village population was African American, and roughly a quarter of them were living on public assistance. As fast as white families moved out, black families moved in.

They came from Brooklyn and Queens looking for a better way of life. Newsday did a multi-series story on "The Making of a Ghetto" where it was pointed out the complicit participation of realtors, elected officials, and the county agency for social public assistance. This was a textbook study on how systemic racism created a concrete example of social injustices resulting in a list of social pathologies that harmed the entire community.

By the time we got to the fourth and fifth forums on "Why Johnny Can't Read," the popularity of these events was such that we had to have them in the high school auditorium. When people walked into the auditorium, they immediately saw a large sign above the stage which read Community Forum Sponsored by Memorial Presbyterian Church.

Governor Nelson Rockefeller sent one of his top aides, and the New York Board of Regents sent a representative to serve on a panel that included the local school board. I moderated the discussion. It was a wild night. Everyone felt very passionate about education. It's generally acknowledged that getting a sound education is an essential key to moving out of poverty and achieving one's dreams and aspirations. Newsday covered the event. This forum gave MPC great street cred.

People were asking me how I got the governor to send a representative and as a response, I just smiled. I didn't know the governor or anyone in his office. I simply called his office and sent a letter, and he responded. That's God's grace working. My stature in the community grew almost without me doing anything to earn it. More importantly, I had made lots of friends with local leaders. They trusted me, and I relied on them. The church grew.

I never thought about doing things with the intent of doing it for the sake of church growth. All I knew was that the church was a useful conduit for people to come to Christ Jesus. That's what I wanted. I wanted people to be exposed to the word, and that meant getting them into the church on Sunday.

More than any other racial group, Black people love two things about church worship: One, they love good preaching, and, two, they love great singing. I'm not a great preacher as far as orators go, but I think I am a good communicator from the pulpit. I try to prepare sermons that teach something about the faith journey and something people can use throughout the week and in their personal tribulations. I don't whoop as some black folk like to hear, but the messages are hopefully and prayerfully good fertilizer for one's faith.

The devil is never off duty. He is committed to taking away our joy, our praise, our devotion to our Savior, our service to the Kingdom, and our confidence in being a Christian. If we allow the word to saturate our walk in Christ and if we permit ourselves to be nurtured in the word daily, then we have a great chance of living an abundant life.

My role as a preacher is to teach what the scripture says about how to live a righteous life so we can share our journey with others. People came to MPC and came back again, and then ultimately, they often joined the fellowship. Thank you, Holy Spirit. I could never take credit for what the Holy Spirit was doing.

MUSIC—WE HEAR MUSIC

The second thing that black people love on a Sunday morning worship moment is soul-stirring uplifting music. MPC was not the traditional euro-centric style service practiced by most black Presbyterian congregations. I believe many black Presbyterian congregations fail to grow because they do not engage in a worship style that reflects the black tradition. They try to imitate a culture that's not afro-centric. Hence, they don't grow in numbers. We were blessed to have one of the best musical expressions and best choirs in New York. I mean, we had it going on. People came from long distances to attend Sunday morning worship at Memorial, from Queens, Brooklyn, and even New Jersey. This all happened through a serendipitous conversation with one of our members, who told me that she had heard that a great musician was looking to move to another church situation. I got his phone number and called.

In 1973 the MPC choir had about seven to nine members, and they were used to singing traditional hymns almost exclusively. As a Baptist preacher, I wanted more upbeat music with a little more energy. I tried for more than a year to get the Session to select a new musician, but they wouldn't budge. I tried to convince them that we'd have a more powerful worship moment if we had a stronger music presence. Finally, they agreed. I was told that another local church had a music director who was interested in moving to another situation. His name was Dr. Stanley Ralph. He came to us in 1976 and stayed with us until 2006, 30 years.

Initially, his coming caused some concern among some of the elders of the church. At the time, we were stronger financially, but still weak as I was making only $65 per week. He was asking for $75 per week.

Their reaction was, "No way are we going to pay our minister of music more than we're paying our pastor." That was my signal to ask for a raise, but I didn't, of course. I had a secular job, and I knew we could not afford to lose Dr. Ralph. Dr. Ralph did more than we could have hoped for or imagined. Within short order, our choir grew. It grew to twenty, then over time to thirty and eventually to more than fifty voices. Plus, he developed a youth choir, a men's chorus, and a women's chorus. Over the years, our choir produced two CDs, sang at the International Choral Fest in Havana, Cuba (2000), and sang with me in Brussels, Belgium and France (1996). He was a genius who could play virtually any genre of church music, hymns, spirituals, gospels, contemporary, and praise. Most important, he was a genuinely decent man who loved the Lord and was committed to the ministry at MPC.

More than serving as our Minister of Music, Dr. Ralph was a partner in ministry. Dr. Ralph was charismatic, entertaining, and personable even when not sitting at the piano or organ. He spoke with authority and commanded the room when he walked in. Everyone respected Dr. Stanley Ralph. We worked exceptionally well together. He was my prayer partner and also a big brother. He was my confidant, and I was his. I officiated his daughter's wedding, Sheryl Lee Ralph, the actress. She flew us down to Kingston, Jamaica, for the service. Several movie stars were there, Denzel Washington, the most prominent.

In 1985, I was invited to attend a world church event in Seoul, South Korea. Dr. Ralph and his wife, Ivy, went with me and my wife, Marie. On the way to South Korea, we spent several days in Tokyo, Japan.

Marie had recently completed a protocol of chemical therapy for her breast cancer and relished the chance to see another part of the world for personal reasons. In 1987, Mr. Raymond Massello, a principle in the tour company, Journey's Unlimited, called me and asked if I'd be interested in attending a World Peace Conference in Jordan and Israel. We'd be gone for twelve days. All expenses were paid. I asked if I could bring my Minister of Music, and he said yes. That was the first of three trips that Dr. Ralph and I would take to Israel and Jordan. We always took members from the church and community. Fifty-five was the highest number of people to travel with us.

If we provide the labor, God provides the increase.

Someone said that when a pastor is before God, he talks about the people. When he is before the people, he talks about God. This is true. In my years of pastoring, I always found myself thinking about how I could better serve the community and the congregation. I discovered that God has a sense of humor. He was working even when I didn't know it. One such blessing came in an unlikely way.

In 1976, Mr. Allard Lowenstein of Long Beach, Long Island, was running for congress. He had invited Mrs. Coretta Scott King, his longtime friend, to come to Long Island to campaign on his behalf. I got a call from the Lowenstein campaign office asking if MPC would host her coming to Long Island. I was surprised that we'd be asked to host a meeting where Mrs. King would be speaking.

Our church was one of the most unlikely venues. It was small, in poor condition, and not well known for this kind of thing. The call could have gone to any number of other pastors, but it came to me. Of course, I said yes. When she came, all the local papers covered her coming. This small church, which at that time held only about 100 people with extra chairs in the aisle, was packed beyond capacity. The basement and outside the church were stacked with people from the community. Mr. Lowenstein spoke, but Mrs. King stole the evening. Her coming gave us additional influence.

A few months later, Rev. Jesse Jackson came to speak on

the issue of voter registration and voter turnout. Again, large crowds gathered and, the newspapers were eager to cover the event. Our reputation grew. However, this time something had changed for me with my fellow pastors. I began to notice two conflicting responses. One response was of appreciation that Jesse came to MPC. The second response was not-so-subtle envy or resentment that he didn't come to one of their churches.

I know this because a couple of the pastors told me so in confidence. More and more people began showing up in the church. Every Sunday, we had to place additional chairs in the aisle. We couldn't use the balcony because structurally, it was not safe. This is before we built our first building.

DEPENDENCE AND INDEPENDENCE

Sometime in 1976, Rev. Bill Rambo, the Executive Presbyter of Long Island (like a bishop of sorts) and a man whom I loved and respected, invited me to lunch. During lunch, he said, "Reggie, I've got some great news for you. The Mission Council voted last week to give Memorial church $10,000 to help what we see going on there." This was significant because just three years earlier, the Presbytery had voted to close the doors of the church, so they stopped all financial aid coming to the church.

Neither I, nor the church got any subsidy from the larger church since that vote.

We were a black congregation with no money and little possibility of growing. We were on our own. By any man's logic, we should have folded and closed our doors, but God had another plan.

We were growing and gaining strength daily. I said to Rev. Rambo, "Please convey to the Mission Council that I and we appreciate the gift of $10,000, but that we don't want the money." Looking shocked, he said, "You don't need $10,000?"

I told him we needed $10,000 and much, much more, but not *that* $10,000. I told him that since we were left to go on our own, the congregation was growing and paying our bills on time. I was concerned that if we were to take the $10,000 that it would usher us back to a paradigm of being on the dole from the Presbytery. I didn't want the church to feel dependent on external financial aid when we could very well take care of our own interests. He was a little shaken but said he understood and would take this message back to the Mission Council.

When I met with the ruling Elders at Memorial a few days later and told them about the lunch, their initial reaction was, "You did what! You turned down $10,000!" When I told my rationale, they hesitantly accepted the decision and felt proud of themselves. We had to be independent when it came to our own efforts but dependent on God and not the largess of the Presbytery. The congregation felt even more proud of our decision and was even more committed to the work of service to the Kingdom of God on earth. They trusted my leadership, and we all trusted God's word.

TITHING

I always tithe. From my first job sweeping hair off the barber's floor and every job since, I'd always given at least 10% of my income to the work of the church. As I got older, I contributed more than 10%. Memorial, like most other Presbyterian churches, conducted an every-member pledge drive to determine what the annual budget would be in the coming year.

When I first arrived at MPC in May of 1973, I discontinued the practice of seeking annual financial pledges from members because it was not an effective way of establishing a meaningful budget. First, the church never got enough money pledged to support even a modest budget. Second, many people failed to honor their pledges and when members failed to honor pledges, what options remain? We can't garnishee their income, and we're not about to ask them to leave the church. So, what's left? We love them and keep moving on. Why did the church conduct these annual pledge campaigns? Because they had always done it, I was told.

I asked the Session to consider us becoming a tithing church. I underestimated their initial reaction. Wow, did they push back. One elder announced in a Session meeting that tithing is Old Testament theology. Jesus didn't teach tithing. We should rely on seeking pledges as we had always done.

It took several meetings, but finally, with the Holy Spirit's aid, the elders agreed we should become a tithing church. I told them fundraising was not biblical. Selling cakes, chicken, and fish dinners, and having fashion shows were not consistent with scripture. You cannot find one place in all the Bible where God or a prophet told the people to go out and organize cake sales or fish fries for the purpose of raising money to sustain the temple. I cited several places in scripture where tithing is mandated. It is not an option. "The tithe is the Lord's."

After the Session approved that we officially become a tithing church, I suggested we hold a meeting with the congregation so all members would understand the importance of tithing. We held the meeting, and the vote passed, but not before that same elder got up in church and publicly embarrassed me by saying I was wrong, I was moving the church in the wrong direction, and that he and his wife were not going to tithe. This same elder left the church in protest when I pushed for us to build a new and larger church building. He said, "Reverend Tuggle is going to put us in debt and then leave us for another more lucrative situation." Even after his speech, the congregation voted overwhelmingly to become a tithing church. I then spent three months preaching and teaching on tithing every Sunday. If the people truly understood the rationale for tithing, they would respond, and wow, did they! Our weekly giving went up four-fold. When I arrived, our annual budget was $12,000 with a little fewer than 40 members. **When I retired as pastor of the Memorial Presbyterian Church, our annual budget was $1,000,000 with nearly 1000 members.**

When I arrived, we had a staff of four including the Minister of Music, part-time secretary, Sexton, and me. When I left, we had a staff of eleven including a full-time and part-time associate pastor and church administrator. When I retired, the church had more than one million dollars in the bank, the mortgage paid off, and no outstanding bills. We did all this by the grace of God and the steadfast support and prayers of all the members. In all my years at MPC, I never begged for money.

I orchestrated two successful capital campaigns to build and complete two buildings (sanctuaries, social halls, office space) without harping on the money every week. My style was to lift up what scripture says about money, particularly about how to support the church financially. The single most talked about subject in the New Testament is how people relate to money or material things. Often people get caught up with the power of money and wealth in such a way that they cannot see the sovereignty of God or the real purpose of money itself. Money should never dominate our faith or our willingness to serve. Money is a tool to be used for one's needs and wants and not for us to be controlled by it. God has already blessed us with health, eyesight, hearing, the ability to walk, talk, and have family and friends, employment, and much more. As it says in II Corinthians 12:9, "My grace is sufficient for you..." We already have more than enough. Once members of the congregation understood the place money plays in God's Kingdom and how they were being blessed by God with so much more than money itself, they were eager to give. Tithing isn't about giving money as much as it is about showing gratitude for what God has done already and willingly submitting to God's lordship over one's life.

WE MUST BUILD

By the end of my first year at MPC, it was clear I wasn't going to leave anytime soon. My stated two-year plan disappeared. I reasoned that God sent me to Memorial for a purpose, and I felt inclined to play it out. Looking back over my life, this is the reason I was born. The reason I was led to go to New York. The reason I worked with migrant workers. To serve in this circumstance. There was just too much work to do. Thirteen years before the release of the fabled movie *Field of Dreams* was made in 1992 with the signature line, "If you build it, they will come," we had the same vision.

In 1976, MPC was showing significant rapid growth. We knew we had to build a bigger church. We had grown from fewer than forty members to more than 100, and our budget had grown as well. We placed extra chairs in the sanctuary every Sunday but still couldn't keep up with the growth. For more than a year, the Session discussed building another church, but it would require lots of money. My vision was to build a church with a seating capacity of 500, but the Presbytery wouldn't support that vision. I told them if we failed now to build a church much larger than where we were at the time, we'd be failing future generations. We had to strike while the iron was hot. We had people, enthusiasm, growing ministries, and significant faith in God to work on our behalf. But the denominational powers didn't see it. They still saw us through the lens of being black, poor, and impotent.

We ended up building a church that would seat at best 190 people and with extra chairs in the aisles would seat an additional thirty to forty people. While we appreciated the fact that we had a new building, I was bitterly disappointed in its size. Again, I felt the lack of support from the white denomination was largely because we were black. My enthusiasm to work within the Presbytery was diminished and remained so throughout my time on Long Island. They had no vision and no faith in us to make this new church become a reality in spite of the evidence that we were growing and doing so at a pace that exceeded all other congregations on Long Island.

The story, as to exactly how our new building came to be, deserves additional comment. I mentioned earlier some of the social and community events MPC conducted that sparked massive interest in the church, but the underpinning was a deliberate focus on Bible study. When I began teaching Bible study in 1973, I would get maybe three to seven people attending. By 1976, we'd get about thirty to forty coming out every week. Over time, we grew to more than 200 attending weekly, with Bible classes being offered seven days per week.

I taught only one class on Thursday nights, and elders taught the others. Ms. Terri Simonson (Allen) came to me and said that since we were placing such a strong emphasis on Bible study, it should be offered seven days a week. We sat down and designed a way for that to happen. Without one's faith anchored in the word, doubts, fears, and a lack of self-confidence creep into one's worldview.

We were all excited about the prospect of building a new church building. So, organizing a capital campaign was relatively easy. There was no need to spend time explaining the reasons why a new building was necessary, it was evident all around us. The tithing initiative was conducted simultaneously with the effort to raise additional money for the capital project. I found an architect who gave the building committee and Session professional guidance on what would be required and for a fee that was well below his standard charge. After getting input from the congregation and the building committee as to what type of building we wanted to meet the many ministry ideas we were providing, Mr. Ed Dickman had a rendering made in living color and mounted on a 4x5 feet board. We placed it in front of the sanctuary for all to see. It was stunning.

Building the new church defied all the predictions about us, a poor black congregation worshiping in a dilapidated structure with precious little money in our pockets. And to make the project even more unlikely, it was a Presbyterian congregation where most of the community citizens were of other denominations. It reminded me of the childhood poem of the little engine that could.

The little blue engine looked up at the hill.
His light was weak, his whistle was shrill.
He was tired and small, and the hill was tall.
And his face blushed red as he softly said,
I think I can, I think I can, I think I can.

So, he started up with a chug and a strain,
And he puffed and pulled with might and main,
And slowly he climbed, a foot at a time
And his engine coughed as he whispered soft,
I Think I can, I think I can, I think I can

With a squeak and a creak and a toot and a sigh,
With an extra hope and an extra try,
He would not stop-now he neared the top-
And strong and proud he cried out loud,
I think I can, I think I can, I think can

In the poem, the engine didn't quite make it to the top. He slid down with a "crash, smash, bash" on the rocks below. But in our case, the members at MPC did have enough faith in God, in themselves, and in the vision. We actually got to the top of the hill.

God sent us another angel. Mr. Ira Hamilton, a black contractor who built the new Memorial and completed the job just two months longer than anticipated and only $31,000 over budget. For those who may not realize how significant this feat is, just know that for any capital project to be finished on time and within budget is extremely rare. I learned so much about how to read blueprints to go along with my ability to read people and how to read the scriptures.

It takes a lot of patience and many prayers to move the church forward during the building process. As time went on, some folks began to express some displeasure with this or that or the other and with me at times. But most people were upbeat and very positive.

Their pride in what we were doing was evident throughout the community as they began to vigorously invite others to come to the church where they could grow spiritually. They'd hear memorable sermons and wonderful uplifting music. People began pouring into the church on Sundays, and with more people came more needs to be met by the church.

We moved into the new Memorial Presbyterian Church in 1979, and we outgrew the seating capacity by 1981. This infuriated me because I knew it would happen. I saw God's plan for growth back in 1976, but I could not convince the Presbytery to go along with us for constructing a larger building. When visiting the church today, one would see two buildings made from the same brick but are so oddly aligned that one would think the architect was either drunk or had failed architecture 101. But what we have is what we had to work with due to the timing of property acquisitions at various stages of building process.

Initially, we didn't have enough land to build the larger building. So, we had to raise money to purchase three houses adjacent to our church just to tear them down for land use. The building department required us to provide a certain number of parking spaces for more off-street parking. When two of our neighbors knew of our interest in purchasing their homes, they raised their price. However, one neighbor, in an act of kindness that I shall always remember, lowered their price, and donated an additional lot next to his house to the cause. This is human nature, and I guess some people are not as gracious as others. God's grace was ever-present.

So, to compensate for the welcomed additional people, we started having two services on Sundays at 8:00 AM and 11:00 AM. Now I was preaching two sermons per week and still working as a solo pastor and working a secular job. I had precious little personal time and used as much of it as I could to give to my wonderful family.

At first, attendance at the new 8:00 AM service was sparse, probably about forty to fifty people. We had agreed to not have less quality in the first service in terms of music and sermon. We'd have ushers and youth participation. The choir was faithfully singing every Sunday at both services, thanks to the leadership of Dr. Stanley Ralph. At first, neither Dr. Ralph nor I accepted any additional compensation for our giving additional work. We agreed that we wanted to see the church's coffers grow. At the beginning of our second year, the Session gave us a raise in pay to reflect our growing congregation and as an expression of their gratitude for our "generous" service.

Within four years, we were able to completely pay off the mortgage for the new building. In 1981, we initiated a second capital campaign to build yet another much larger church building. In nine years, the congregation raised a million dollars above and beyond our regular operations budget by relying on tithing, plus members gave extra out of their savings or other sources. We raised funds through fashion shows, cruises, dinner-dances, and youth group car washes. The men also held fish and chicken dinner sales. Mind you, none of the funds raised for the building project was used for church operations and ministry programs. That was all done through tithing. So, there was no contradiction in our pledge to run the church entirely on the strength of tithes. In fact, we kept building funds completely separate from the general operating fund accounts.

On April 1, 1990, we moved into the newer MPC that would seat nearly 500 people. It was a grand hallelujah day as we marched from one church building to another. I lead the march, followed by the Ruling Elders, then the oldest members among us, then the youth, then all others.

Also, during this time, we were increasing the amount of money going to mission causes. The Presbytery was complimentary of our giving to mission causes even though they were not that supportive in the early days. When we went to them for support to build the first building, they would only give us a $38,000 loan subject to repayment after the commercial loan had been liquidated.

We asked for much more than they were willing to give. We paid off the commercial loan in three years and the Presbytery about 18 months later with interest. By 1996, MPC had paid off all mortgage obligations. This was remarkable. There is good news, and then there is God-news. This is GOD-NEWS. The congregation kept on growing. Thank you, Holy Spirit!

MINISTRY IS SERVICE

Churches are conduits through which the gospel message is delivered, but we also must be responsive to the social, emotional, and spiritual needs of the community and congregants. **Churches should be open for service seven days a week.**

One of the great failings of the local congregation is that it sees itself often as a Sunday only morning place of worship and service. All churches have some resources, and those resources should be used to enrich and enhance the quality of life of the community. Larger churches with larger congregations have a greater responsibility to do more than smaller ones. To whom much is given, much is required. This is true, but it's easier to say than to do. I have always argued that the biggest impediment to ministry isn't the lack of money, but the lack of faithful people willing to serve the needs of Jesus Christ through the channels of the church. It's not the lack of money that results in the absence of ministry, but the lack of people. Human capital is the single most important feature of providing ministry. The way to increase the number of people willing to step up and do more is what pastors are called to teach. We preach, but we also teach and motivate and model what we preach. We give a clear rationale for what has to be done and then stimulate action to accomplish the defined objectives.

Johnathan Swift, the 18th-century author, and essayist said that great leaders are those who have a vision and are clever enough to paint a picture of it so plainly that others can also see it. I don't have many skills, but I believe one of my skills is to paint pictures so others can see them. If one can see it, one can move in the direction of achieving it. If the congregation can't see it, it can't believe it's possible. The essential key to remember that forward movement isn't possible until a large majority of the congregation can see it. Otherwise, there will be strife.

There has to be an assessment of the physical, financial, and spiritual needs of the congregation. People's emotional strength and complexities have to be addressed because many are living with brokenness—broke in spirit, broken in various relationships, broke in their relationship with God. Then, once ministry programs have been established internally to address these matters, the second more aggressive task must be launched, and that is to look at the needs of the external community and see what, how, and where the church can play a healing role. Ministry programs should never be enacted in a vacuum.

We should avoid busy work for the sake of having activities at the church. It has to have some meaningful connection to the pain and suffering of neighbors or to the building of closer bonds among members. Further, the church isn't a social agency focusing only on shelter, food, education, health, jobs, and crime. Yes, we must address these things, but first and last, we are a gospel promoting institution where our primary concern is for people's salvation. The church is, or should be, the place where the love of Christ is first manifested among the members of the congregation. If disciples of Jesus fail to see themselves as brothers and sisters of Christ and act in a loving way towards each other, those looking in on the church from the outside will not be able to hear our salvation message. We don't represent Christ well when we act in unloving ways; God's Kingdom suffers.

IT'S NOT THE BUILDING BUT THE PEOPLE.

People don't go to a particular church because of its facility, its building. No matter how beautiful the structure, if the people in it are not suited for demonstrating the love of Christ, then visitors won't stay and most assuredly will not invite others to come. People design, establish, and execute all the expressions of ministry. This was our success story, if I may use this expression. I say this advisedly because nowhere in scripture did God tell the church to go out into the world and be successful. He told the church to be faithful, in season and out of season.

Our efforts are evaluated by a different set of standards based on how people are saved to the salvation of Jesus Christ, how their lives are changed for the better, and how the external community is improved. To that end, MPC established many ministries over the years. The following represent years of energy and faithful service by many people:

- Bible Study—offered seven days a week. Youth Bible Study every Friday evening and Men's Bible Study every Saturday morning, Seniors every Wednesday at noon, Evangelism courses every Sunday afternoon at 4:00 PM and nightly at 7:00 PM.

- Music Ministry—Chancel choir every Wednesday at

7:00 PM, Youth Choir Saturday at 1:00 PM, Men's Chorus and Women's Chorus as needed, The church music department incorporated drums, organ and piano, and sometimes saxophone and percussion instruments, on special occasions violins, trumpets, and bass.

- Women's League—for all women in the church, but only about 50-70 actively participated. They did a variety of wonderful things, such as, work with our youth, host picnics, arrange outings to Broadway plays, work in nursing homes, raise money for the scholarship fund and building fund, Bible study, host coffee hour after Sunday worship, organize annual spiritual retreats, etc.

- Fifty-five Plus Club—for all members aged 55 and older. They brought in experts to speak on topics of interest to the elderly such as living on a fixed income, stroke prevention, diet, how to build healthy relationships with grown children and grandchildren, annuities, trusts, living wills, etc. They also went to plays, the beach, and of course, Bible study. There was more than 100 active participants and many non-church members also participated.

- Prison Ministry—members went to the county jail on a weekly basis. Many of our new members came from this effort. At its peak, as many as fifteen regular adults participated in this ministry.

- Men's Council—for all men of the church but only approximately 30-40 men actively participated. They conducted Bible study, worked with the youth, sponsored spiritual retreats, organized bonding activities for themselves and for non-church men in the community, prison ministry, etc.

- Youth Ministry—for all youth in the church. Activities included basketball games with youth of other churches, skating events, Broadway plays, NY Mets and NY Yankees baseball games, etc.

- Charmettes—for girls ages 5-11. Activities included arts and crafts, breakfasts every Saturday, outings, Bible study.

- Charm—for girls ages 12-18. Met every Saturday. Activities were grooming, etiquette, arts and crafts, sexuality (for the older girls), how to interview for a job, book study, Bible study, one-on-one discussions on topics of interests to the girls, etc.

- Manhood Training Program—for boys 8-15. The group met every Saturday and each boy was assigned a man for mentoring, coaching, and modeling what it meant to be a responsible Christian man. Activities included going to the nursing home monthly to read to the residents or listen to their life stories, attending ball games, Bible study, one-on-one discussions on topics of interest to boys

- Pathway—a grant from the Pathway foundation for $200,000 for certain youth who demonstrated severe behavioral problems. Nearly all of these participants came as referrals from the public junior and senior high school. These youth were candidates for school drops. They received even more intense one-on-one counseling. The youth got a $50 stipend every three months, and upon graduation, got a $10,000 grant for college expenses. If they chose not to go to college, they could use the money for trade school. Or if they didn't want to do that, they could have access to the funds after five years for use as a down payment on a house, or they could use the funds to go into business once the business plan was approved by a committee of businessmen.

- After-school Tutoring—for any student in church or the community needing remedial attention in Math or English. Our teachers were retired teachers or interested adults wanting to tutor. Available Monday through Thursdays from 3-6 PM. The church provided snacks such as cookies, milk, and water.

- Youth Bible Study—every Friday night for youth church members and community youth.

- Memorial Youth Outreach—a 501c3 organization that operated programs in a neighboring building and funded by the county. Services provided by a staff of four, five days a week. Funded by the church and a county grant.

- Ushers—for adult ushers and youth.

- Sunday School—for all youth and adults.

- Alcoholics Anonymous—met twice weekly.

- Narcotics Anonymous—met once weekly.

- Feed My Sheep Ministry—a food ministry where we passed out non-perishable food every Saturday to community members. Food was provided by the members of the church and the local supermarket.

- Memorial Economic Development Corp.—a 501c3 ministry designed to promote and conduct economic development in the Roosevelt Community, funded by the church and various grants from foundations, government, and corporate.

- Deacons—a ministry of benevolence for all sick and ailing people conducted by the deacons. Home and hospital visitations were part of the growth of the church.

- Service to the grieving and for preparing repast meals after a funeral event. Met twice monthly.

Chapter 11

GOING HOME FOR A BLESSING

After a couple of years of serving at Memorial, I went back to Denver to visit my mother for a few days. Some of the elders had expressed concerns that I hadn't taken a Sunday off in nearly three years. "We want you to stay around a while, so don't burn yourself out. Take some time off."

A couple of days after I arrived, my mother's friend and a longtime acquaintance of mine as well, invited us to her house for dinner. I met her daughter, Marie Rebecca Peoples, at the dinner. She's the woman I used to play with, along with her two brothers, when we were kids. Our reunion was serendipitous. Marie was divorced and I was single. After about a year's worth of courting over the phone, writing letters along with some exchange visits, I was convinced she was the person God sent for me to marry. She met all the criteria necessary to be a pastor's wife, or more specifically, this pastor's wife. She was already active in her church, loved the Lord, was humble, loving, generous, and good at managing money.

We got married in 1976 in the old, dilapidated structure of a church, had our reception in the social hall at Freeport Presbyterian Church, a much nicer place, and then honeymooned in the Pocono Mountains of Pennsylvania. She accepted her role as the first lady, although I didn't place much stock in the title. Neither of us did.

Marie was a great partner. She taught Sunday School, sang in the choir, and was also active in the Women's League. People loved her, and she loved them back. Having an extraordinary skillset in arts and crafts, she was always doing things with her hands. Part of this ability was due to her majoring in home economics in college. She once made a Sunday suit for me from scratch. She also made some of her own dresses, and when our daughters were born, she made their dresses, too. Professionally, she worked as a social worker at the county's drug and alcohol department, a job similar to the one she had in Denver. Her mother owned several houses in Denver and had taught Marie how to purchase property. When we married, Marie owned three houses, including the one she lived in.

She understood finance and didn't mind my rather extreme money management habits. I lived and died by the budget. If something wasn't in the budget, we didn't buy it. We agreed on three things when we were married. First, all the money she'd earn would be hers. I would pay the bills for the household, and if she wanted to contribute to those bills, it would be welcomed. (She often contributed to the bills.) Second, I asked her to tithe to the work of the church and she did. Third, I asked that she save at least the same amount she was giving to the church for her own use. Expenses beyond that, such as her credit card bills, were hers, not mine. The formula worked for us.

Both of us had an interest in owning rental property. We began looking around for suitable property with a positive cash flow to invest our money left after expenses. I had owned rental properties before, in Denver and Florida, but this time, it would be with a partner. After looking for more than a year, we found a 42-unit elevator building in Flatbush, Brooklyn. It was priced beyond our reach, but I thought with a little luck, we could make it work.

By my analysis, the building could be a cash cow for us if we managed it well and if the tenants paid their rent on time. I let my irrational enthusiasm blind me from reality. I went ahead and bought the building against the advice of my lawyer. The lawyer had warned me that I didn't have enough experience managing a building of that size and the courts in New York were not landlord friendly. Arrogance took over me, and we purchased the building. To make the purchase possible, I needed all of Marie's savings combined with mine as a down payment. She was a little reluctant to contribute all of her savings to this venture, but I guaranteed her that she'd get every penny back with interest if it didn't work out.

We created an LLC in both our names and purchased the building. Within three months, the plan began to show significant deficiencies. In short, it fell completely apart. The boiler broke down, tenants' needs grew, and some renters stopped paying rent due to being laid off, losing their jobs, or illness.

It was one nightmare after another. Even after hiring a full-time building superintendent, I found myself having to drive to Brooklyn, a forty-five minute to one hour drive, once or more each week. My phone never stopped ringing. My lawyer's advice, which I ignored, echoed in my memory over and over again. I learned the lesson. DON'T IGNORE SOUND ADVICE! Proverbs says that a fool spurns wise counsel.

I was at my wit's end and didn't quite know what to do. We considering filing for bankruptcy but it would have a negative impact on us for years to come, so that was a non-starter. I tried holding on for a few more months, but things just got worse. Finally, a little less than a year into this quagmire, I told Marie I'd had enough and started looking for a buyer. At first, I just wanted back what we had put into the actual purchase, but I was happy to even get a little less as time went on. However, the offer we agreed on was a lot less than what we hoped for. The people who bought the property were professionals, and I didn't stand a chance of negotiating with them. We ended up losing virtually all of our savings, but we were free of this albatross hanging around our necks. Hallelujah!

Marie was very disappointed, but not as much as I was. I had let her down. Buying the building was my idea, and she trusted me with her resources to help make it happen. I told her that I'd return all of her savings with interest after some time. In the meanwhile, I told her I wanted us to give more money to the church. She replied, "You already give more than 10% to the church, and now in the wake of this loss, you want to give more?" "This is precisely what the devil wants to do...to make us give less in the way of the Lord," I told her. So, we increased our giving to the church.

VITO VALONE

At Yale, I had developed the habit of going to the gym several days a week to ease the mental stress and keep my energy level up. On Long Island, I went to Echo Park Recreation Center in West Hempstead, a 25-meter indoor and outdoor pool, a weight room, and a sauna and steam room. My routine was to swim twenty laps of the pool, spend ten min on weight lifting and fifteen minutes in the sauna, and take a shower and leave. Over the years of going there, I had become friendly with Vito Valone, a regular who worked at E.F. Hutton, a large brokerage Wall Street firm.

One day, while we were sitting in the sauna, I shared with him my tale of woe about the apartment building. He told me that the market was poised to enter a bull market cycle and that if I worked with him, he thought that in a few years, we could make a substantial return on investment. I agreed to do this. We had lunch twice a month for several months, and he taught me a lot about the market. It took about four years, but I had earned enough to return back Marie's money. Thank you, Vito. Thank you, Lord.

I planned a creative way to return Marie's money. I made reservations at a fancy restaurant and took a gift-wrapped package to the maître d' de earlier that day. As dessert was being served, the maître d' brought a gift-wrapped package and gave it to my wife. She curiously looked at the man and then the gift and asked, "What is this?" He told her exactly what I had instructed him to say.

"Madam, a gentleman told me to give this to you, and then he walked away." She opened the package and found a leather pouch containing all cash. It was the return of all her investment in the apartment building plus interest. She was overwhelmed and shouted, "Oh, my goodness! I don't believe this." She then jumped up and came to give me a big hug, and then we both laughed and enjoyed our dinner together. I received more hugs when we reached home. I felt better because God had enabled me to keep my promise to my wife, by His grace.

Chapter 12

THE JOY, PRIDE, & LOSS

Marie and I both wanted children, and tried for about three years with no positive results. Marie suggested we try to adopt, but I wanted my own biological children and refused the idea for a long time. Later, we were referred to a fertilization clinic at the North Shore hospital. I will never forget our first visit to the facility and what we heard in the doctor's presentation on childless couples wanting to have children. I had to produce sperm for analysis, and she had to take fertility pills. More than a year passed, and still, there were no positive results. Later, I finally agreed to start the process of adoption. The following month, Marie became pregnant, Praise God, we celebrated that night. The doctor told us that this kind of event happens more commonly than science can understand. After a childless couple finally agrees to adopt, the wife becomes pregnant. It's not uncommon, but it is unexpected.

On February 11, 1980, our firstborn, Karleena Regina-Marie Tuggle, came into the world. She was born five and a half weeks early and weighed less than six pounds. Earlier that Sunday, we had just come from an afternoon service at a local Baptist church. Their worship style was to have extremely loud music. Marie was placed in a seat near the huge speakers. The bass was so loud it made one's whole body shake with the beat and caused one's ears to hurt. She wasn't used to this. Later that evening, she began having cramps. We called the doctor, and he attributed the cramps to Braxton Hicks, physical cramping experienced by women in late pregnancy. He told us to relax and call him again if the cramping got worse and the contractions became more frequent.

The cramping got worse. I called the doctor, and he said, "Rush her to the hospital." I tried getting her off the bed, but she could barely walk. With some considerable effort, we got her downstairs and into the back seat of the car. I felt as though I was driving 100 miles per hour at about 1:30 in the morning.

When we got to the hospital, I rushed into the emergency room, yelling, "My wife is having a baby, help!" A nurse came to the car, took one look under Marie's robe, and shouted for a wheelchair. When I got to the delivery room, I was told I had to put on proper clothing. I rushed, but by the time I got to the delivery room, the baby was on her way out into the world. Marie still had her glasses on. I got there just in time for the doctor to reach in for the baby and pull her out, and then, after a brief clearing of our baby's breathing passages, she placed her in my arms. I was overwhelmed with indescribable exhilaration. The time of birth, as recorded by the hospital, was 2:18 AM. Coincidentally, the address of our home was 218 Hudson Ave., Freeport, New York. To this day, I attribute that loud church music to Karleena's early arrival.

As I looked into the eyes of this beautiful child, I had no idea of what she'd become. I didn't know that twenty-five years later, she would graduate from Howard University Medical School, then five years later, Dr. Karleena R. M. Tuggle would be a board-certified surgeon. Today she is the chief bariatric surgeon and medical director at a regional hospital in Atlanta, Georgia, and a Lt. Colonel in the U.S. Army Reserve.

On November 28, 1983, our second child, Regine Perry Tuggle, was born. Her birth wasn't quite as dramatic as her sister's but just as exciting. Marie carried the baby nearly full-term, but I was more than a bit excited on the morning of delivering the baby. I called in Mother Ruth Greif, the only white member at MPC at the time and one of the oldest. She adopted me as a son, and I called her Mom. It was to her house that I took Karleena in the early hours of November 28. Regine came into the world with practically no complications. What an incredibly gorgeous baby. Regine would become a scholar. She graduated from Florida A&M University with high honors and a master's degree in business. Today she is a mid-level executive for a major retail's worldwide operation.

For years, I carried a picture of a can of Pride furniture cleaner in my wallet along with a can of Joy furniture wax. When I'd go to places, and people exchanged introductions,

I waited for the question to come up, "Well, do you have children?" This was my chance to show off pictures of my Pride and Joy. They would be looking for me to display pictures of my children, but I showed them an actual picture of Pride & Joy. They'd be caught off guard, and we'd all get a healthy laugh. But the truth remains, Karleena and Regine are my Pride and Joy.

THE DARKEST DAY

Marie was an incredibly beautiful woman, and we had a fantastic marriage for sixteen years. Less than a year of Regine's birth, Marie was diagnosed with stage four breast cancer. This beautiful woman, the mother of our children, was just thirty-two years old. When we were told the prognosis and the proposed treatment plan, I couldn't see anything. I felt as if I was temporarily blind, quite literally. I was numb. Marie was stoic at first and devastated later. We cried, prayed together, and then worked together to overcome the crisis. Marie's mother flew out from Denver to assist with the children. She took great care of everything and brought stability to the household. After a couple of months, she returned to Denver, so the three of us discussed what to do with our daughters. Karleena was just starting school and was pretty much self-sufficient. She could dress and feed herself and was already disciplined in studying. Marie had done an incredible job in training the children and giving them a keen sense of self-confidence.

Regine was younger, barely a toddler, and required more attention and nurturing. Marie recommended her mother take Regine back to Denver for a short time while she was getting used to the chemotherapy protocol. I didn't want it to be this way, but I also knew I didn't have the resources to look after Marie, Karleena, and Regine. At the same time, I still pastored and worked at Newsday. My world was turned upside down. I was miserable and depressed but had to give the outward appearance that all was well, or at least manageable. For a long time, I didn't feel much of anything. I felt as though I was going through the transitions of being awake, but was emotionally drifting from one event, one meeting, and one conversation to the next. When people come to church, they come to worship God and to give thanks. They don't come to have that experience impeded by having to look up and see a pastor in distress. So, I acted as though things were better than they actually were.

After surgery, Marie's trial began in earnest. First, in getting used to her new body, and then the chemo's side effects. I tried to be as encouraging as I could. Both of us were optimistic about the long-term outcome, and we lived with a lot of joy in our home. God was so good to her, and she gave us a large measure of that goodness through her smiles and hugs. Our marriage took on a new oneness. I took her to nearly all of her appointments to see the doctor, and when I couldn't, members of the church helped. Jeanette and

Charles Suit, Mrs. Freddie Ashby, Mrs. Angela Archer, Barbara and Bunny Young, Bunny Frisby, Dorothy Wilson, Val Stackhouse, Joseph and Gladys Gabeau, and many others. They also helped with food preparation and sometimes would take Karleena to their homes for short periods.

Through all of this, Marie's courage was a model of a faithful and trusting servant. She rarely complained and would not let anyone come to the house and display a sad face or speak negatively. I remember telling one of our members that she had to leave. She said to her, "I can't take anyone coming to visit me with a sad face and less than hopeful words. You have to go." The person protested, stating that she didn't intend to cause discomfort. But Marie held her ground, "I'm sorry, but you have to go."

Our prayer life was intense, and we believed God would heal her body. Both of us grew stronger spiritually. She told me she always loved me, even as a child. She also told me she liked being around me as a child, but I was always interested in playing with her brothers and ignored her. I loved her so much and couldn't see how I'd respond to life itself if she weren't there. We gained a new relationship with our Creator. It was uplifting to be held by the strength of the Holy Spirit, who shielded us from the crushing fear and anger of her condition. Marie always smiled, but every now and then, I'd catch her looking pensively into the void. Still, she always embraced her children with a strong hug and words of faith.

When Regine returned after nearly two years, she was walking, talking, and happy. Our children's grandmother had done a great job of teaching and nurturing our daughter. She appeared to have no emotional scars from the absence, although I suspect that some scarring had occurred that may still affect her. I felt as if I had lost valuable time with my little lady. Marie and I were so excited to have Regine back with us, and Karleena was over the moon.

While I worked, Marie shared her spirit and her personality with the girls. The girls cultivated a kind of silent strength and confidence that continues to serve them well. They were very bright intellectually and successful academically. They both could read before starting kindergarten. They made As in virtually all subjects throughout kindergarten to grade 12. They attended private Christian schools and we trained them to read the Bible regularly and tried to give them piano lessons, as well, for a couple of years. Though that didn't turn out as we had hoped it would. They tried tennis together, and that worked out better. Regine ran on the school track team and played basketball a little, while Karleena was not an athlete.

Upon graduation from high school, Karleena got the Presidents' Scholarship to Duke University, the Harvard of the South, but turned it down, much to my disappointment. She chose, instead, to take the Meyerhoff Scholarship and attend the University of Maryland Baltimore County. Regine secured admission at Yale University but declined the offer, preferring to go to Florida A&M University on a Presidential Scholarship. I attribute their personal and academic success to their mother's wisdom and, after her passing, to those MPC members who selflessly helped all of us.

HOW COULD YOU, GOD?

The chemo went as well as could be expected, and she completed the protocol after five years. She had a tough time during the sessions, nausea, hair loss, and general fatigue. At one point, Marie was given little hope. But she rebounded, by God's grace. She returned to work as a bank branch manager. The doctors couldn't find any trace of the disease. We celebrated, but it was short-lived. A few months later, cancer had returned, but it was in the brain and liver this time. This was a crushing blow for her and for me. I remember driving home from the doctor's office in complete silence after just hearing the devastating news. Neither of us said a word. What could we even say?

The entire church was informed, and the whole congregation joined in for prayer and fasting. There was a point when the entire congregation fasted for three weeks, surviving on water and juices only. Her recovery became a beacon of hope and trust in God. Marie fought valiantly and always with a smile. Towards the end, we talked about heaven, about the girls, about me, and what it would be like, to finally meet the Creator. On the day she transitioned, she died in my arms while in the doctor's office at 2:00 PM on January 5, 1993. I had known Marie since kindergarten. Now she was gone. She was the wind beneath my wings.

For a long time, I was angry with God. She was just 42, the beautiful mother of our two children with a long life still ahead of her. I mourned for two years. At church, I would pretend as though I was coping with her absence and was alright. I'd often come home from church on Sunday, and when the children weren't looking, find a quiet place in the house and cry in solitude. I had to get used to the void created by her absence. I'd go to work at Newsday and pretend all was well and would get all my reports and assignments done well and on time. Then one day after two years, as I was walking in the yard before going to work, a voice said that *Marie is all right and all is well. Get on with your life.*

NEW BLESSINGS

The primary reason I was able to get involved in so many substantive activities was because my wife provided care and nurture to all of us. She was a remarkable anchor, and she provided Karleena and Regine with wise counseling and mentoring as they transitioned into their teen years. Their mother set the foundation for what was to come later, as they turned into young women. Even now, as adults, they still remember the wonderful and poignant conversations they shared with their mother. I didn't have to worry about how things were going at home, and this gave me tremendous freedom to perform at work and in the life of the church.

ME AND THE GIRLS

Grace has a way of fortifying us in times of weakness. In many ways, after Marie's transition, I felt profoundly lost. So, I did a foolish thing. Instead of spending time mourning properly, taking time off, and focusing on my inner pain, I immersed myself in work. I became a workaholic. Having a social life was almost non-existent, initially.

I grew concerned about how the girls were doing emotionally. Having taken help from members of the church to look after them, do their hair, help with their chores, and kind of being a surrogate parent really helped me a lot. The girls and I took time off to visit Niagara Falls and Toronto for nearly two weeks, cementing a special bond between us. The following summer, we went to England for a week. Exploring London was easy because it's not difficult to get around. There are so many wonderful things to experience— castles, museums, plays, and restaurants.

Several of the following summers, I wanted Karleena and Regine to have as many rich experiences as possible. I wanted the experiences to be different than the norm, something extraordinary. I enrolled Karleena in a language immersion program. She spent two summers in Spain, staying with a family that spoke only Spanish. When Regine got older, she too went to Spain. Later, I took Regine to a summer camp in upstate New York for four summers. This was a camp that spent time each day teaching academics. It specialized in teaching, campers, various elements of circus performance, like trapeze, clowning, juggling, tumbling, and more. They both deepened their self-confidence and their love for adventure.

After graduating from Howard University's medical school, Karleena spent the summer in Quito, Ecuador working in a hospital in order to improve her Spanish medicinal vocabulary. When her six weeks ended, she hired a guide and with a friend, took a canoe down the Amazon River for a couple of days. While in college, Regine spent one summer studying marketing in China at the University of Beijing. Both girls went on to become extraordinarily successful in their respective careers. But more than being successful, they are decent humans. For some reason, I escaped the period where teenagers rebel against parental guidance. They weren't perfect, but they were a joy to be around.

Karleena is now happily married to a hardworking, successful young man, Darian, in Atlanta. Regine is happily married to a great man, Andre, a mid-level executive for a major Fortune 500 company and they have two fantastic children, Isaac (9) and Rebecca (10 months). They are a blessing, a new blessing. Isaac and Rebecca are being groomed to share their God-given gifts with the world and their generation.

Chapter 13

ONE NIGHT IN JERUSALEM

O ver the years, I led church tours to Israel, starting when I first went there in 1987. On my fourth trip, fifty-five people from the church and community went along with me. I always loved going there, the rightly-called "Holy Land" because it gave all visitors an opportunity to witness the Bible come to life.

We walked on the land where our Lord walked. The days used to be filled to capacity. Beginning at 7:30 AM, everyone was given a wonderful traditional Mediterranean breakfast consisting of various salads, fish, juices, eggs, fruits, croissants, and other items such as bread, cereal, coffee, etc. Then we got on buses to see as much of the land as possible in nine days. We visited the Sea of Galilee, Tiberius, Nazareth, Jericho, Masada, The Mt. of Olives, Mt. Zion, many churches, and more. The days were tedious and filled with rich and useful information for one's faith journey. One of my favorite things to do was baptize people in the Jordan River, the river where John The Baptist baptized Jesus. The days were exhausting. When we returned to the hotel, it'd be time for dinner. We'd be briefed about the activities planned for the next day, and then we'd go off to our rooms to rest before the next day's tours.

One night in Jerusalem, I talked to Evette Beckett in the hotel lobby. We talked for a long time. I could see there was something there but couldn't quite put my finger on it.

When we returned to New York, I called her and asked if she and her daughter, Lauren, wanted to go watch *The Brady Bunch Movie*, with my daughters and me. She couldn't go as she had promised the Women's League that she'd help them do something, but we did end up going to see *Braveheart* a few weeks later. For a long time, we used to talk on the phone and got to know each other pretty well. Later I had to break it off because I promised myself I wouldn't marry again until Regine had finished high school. I think, at that time, she was not even in seventh grade.

Evette and I stopped dating for nearly two years. Then one day, I realized she was the woman God had sent down for me to marry. I loved her, and she loved me and my children. Evette had all the qualities I was looking for in a partner. She loved the Lord, was intellectually gifted, adventurous, generous, hardworking, and beautiful. I proposed to her on December 8, 2000 in Bryant Park in Manhattan after having attended a Chase Bank Community Advisory Board meeting. We announced our engagement on December 31 and were married on June 24, 2001.

When I announced to the congregation that I had proposed to Evette, we received a standing ovation. I told the congregation they would all be invited. As a pastor, one could not cherry-pick the invitation list. It would be the kiss of death for the pastor. Either all would be invited or none. As our sanctuary could only hold 500 people at most with extra chairs in the isles, the Catholic Church was gracious enough to allow us to hold the wedding there. We had 1000 people in attendance and *The New York Times* covered the event in their Style section. It was a great day. We honeymooned in France and Italy for nearly two weeks.

Evette and I share a solid marriage, pray together daily, do things that enhance life experiences, travel, and laugh often together. She was involved in the life of the church as a Sunday School teacher, youth leader, praise dance ministry member, and president of the Women's League. Every pastor needs to have a stable home life to perform the work of pastoring effectively. I am blessed, by God's grace, to have Evette in my life. Had she not been on the trip to Israel, we would not have had that fateful talk in Jerusalem.

Evette and I have visited Israel together three times and renewed our vows for our tenth wedding anniversary in the Garden of Gethsemane.

Chapter 14

CHURCH & EDUCATION

By the time I arrived at MPC in 1973. It had a scholarship program that offered $150 to every student who graduated and was going to college. Over the years, God blessed us to increase the dollar amount to $500 per student and later to $1,750 per high school graduate. What that translates into is, if the church had twelve of our students graduate, it would be $1,750 x 12 or $21,000. If we had 25 students graduate, it would be 25 x $1,750 for all students or $43,700. They could also use the money to attend trade schools if they so chose. The church members worked hard all year round raising money for the church's scholarship program. One time, one of our members bequeathed $30,000 to the church for the scholarship fund. It was derived from her father's insurance payment upon his death.

The focus on Education, however, started from elementary school. In Sunday school, we asked teachers to make sure their students had library cards and to review their report cards. We asked them to make sure they encourage students to do well in school. We saw the Sunday school teachers' role as enablers, more than parents, in encouraging students to take Education seriously. Education was a huge focus at Memorial.

THE ROOSEVELT CHILDREN'S ACADEMY

For many years, the Roosevelt community school district was very dysfunctional. The village of Roosevelt was one of the poorest and worst-run school districts in the county and New York State. The high school drop rate was more than 25%, and it scored among the lowest passing rates for students on the Island.

Superintendent turnover was off the scale, with the average superintendent tenure lasting less than two years. This was compounded by the school board which was functioning so inappropriately that at one point, we had three superintendents being paid simultaneously. This happened because when a superintendent who had a three-year contract got terminated before his tenure ended, the district was still obligated to pay for the contract's remaining term even though it hired a new superintendent. This pattern was often repeated. The situation became so bad that the New York State Board of Education, for the first time in state history, disbanded the local school board and took over the district. It was a nightmare, both for students and parents.

Because of our earlier involvement in the school district, MPC was known for its interest in students' welfare. One day, Mr. Robert Francis called for us to have lunch and discuss what we could do to help provide quality education for Roosevelt's students. That lunch resulted in the two of us establishing a charter school, the Roosevelt Children's

Academy. Starting a charter school was expensive and very complicated. We had to do two things immediately. First, find the money and second, complete a detailed (thick) application as required by the New York State Board of Education. As it would turn out, we found a person who fulfilled both needs simultaneously.

We found an extremely wealthy person who was interested in helping us start a charter school. In New York State, charter schools are funded by local school districts that send their students to us to receive education. The formula was quite simple. Charter schools received 2/3 of the per capita dollar allocation per student. For example, if a school district spent $15,000 per student, charter schools would get $10,000 per student. If we got 100 students, we'd receive one million dollars per year from school districts. Our benefactor agreed to pay all expenses for as long as it took to become fully operational. He vouched to pay for all costs, including salaries, rentals, and everything else. Plus, he hired consultants and other needed professionals to complete the application. He agreed to do all of this for a sizeable interest rate on the use of his funds. This was a win-win situation for all of us. As we became more competent in managing the school, we terminated the contract with the benefactor after approximately five years. We opened the school with grades K-3 with a plan to increase grade levels with the pace of one per year until we reached grade 8.

Bob and I served as Board chairman and vice-chairman,

respectively. Then we went about looking for people who were dedicated to educating children with very challenging demographics and who would be interested in serving on the school's Board of Trustees. We ended up with seven of us in total. Once we got the paperwork approved, our application accepted, and our buildings in place, we commenced our operations in 2000. Today, we have 700 students and 130 employees.

Upon opening our doors for the first time, the local school district attacked me, personally, in one of their monthly newsletters. It stated that I was getting rich from the charter school. Of course, it was a lie. No member of the trustee board was allowed to receive any compensation in any form for our services. I was outraged but I did not have to defend myself. Members of the church went to the district superintendent's office and demanded a written public apology, and they got it. The following month, the district published an apology, but it cost me one member of the church, a teacher in the district. She felt charter schools were a threat to her and other teachers. I met her and tried to explain our position, but she wouldn't change her mind and withdrew her membership. Even though I now live in Charlotte, I am still the Academy's Chairman of the Board of Trustees, by God's grace. I am most proud of our accomplishments.

I am humbled to think about what we've accomplished over the years. The demographics of our student population is 98% low-income, black, and Hispanic. Only about 16% of our students have parents who went to college, and all of them are in the free lunch and breakfast program. The majority of our students score low grades when they arrive, but if they stay with us for four or more years, they consistently score much higher than the regular public school district on standardized state tests. To accomplish this, our school day is ninety-minutes longer than the public school, and our teachers don't get tenure contracts.

We have a twelve-million-dollar annual budget with a comfortable reserve. Last year we were able to take our eighth-graders to Ghana, and the year before that, we took them to the African American History Museum in Washington, DC.

In February of 2020, we were successful in getting our fifth five-year unconditional charter renewal, a major accomplishment. All charter schools in New York are certified with only a five-year period before seeking another five-year charter.

The surest way out of poverty is obtaining a quality education that reinforces self-confidence to be able to fulfill one's dream. We want our students to be entrepreneurs, supervisors, and professionals in their chosen field of interest. Most of all, we want them to succeed so they can reach back and help others who are coming up behind them. This is what we teach, this is what we believe. The Roosevelt Children's Academy is blessed with a committed Board of

Trustees which welcomes innovative ideas that produce excellence. Our teaching personnel are devoted to the highest standards of learning and teaching.

Chapter 15

FATHER, WHERE ARE YOU?

At age eighteen, I began looking for my biological father. I found him when I was fifty-eight, forty years later. The quest to find my father was fueled, at first, by hatred for him as he left my mother and me in dire poverty. Had it not been for some key people, who intervened in my life, I would have lost.

When I started my search to find my dad, there was no Internet, no Ancestry.com, no global process to access the data, and no search engines. I only knew his name and that he was, at some point, in the army. I was not a professional at finding people but I wrote letters to the army, asked my relatives what they knew of him, and visited libraries looking for genealogy information. I even inquired in the dead files. However, I didn't search for him all the time, just when the mood hit me and time permitted.

In 1985, I retained the services, pro bono, of Mr. Julius Pearse, a retired detective. He and his wife, Joycetta, had an extensive interest in genealogy and had been quite successful in finding people's ancestors. After hearing my story, he took it as an opportunity to gauge just how good he was at finding people and as a favor to me. Over the next several years, he called me every now and then to tell me he'd found a lead. But upon further investigation, it was usually found to not be of any value.

My mother would ask how I was doing in my search. I think she wanted me to find him as much as I did. One day, while the two of us were having breakfast in a restaurant at a family reunion in California, she asked, "How is the search to find your father going?"

I told her of my many failed attempts. After hearing my stories, she let out a quiet but discernable moan.

"Oh, my God. I am ashamed of myself. Oh, son, I'm so sorry."

I wanted to know what it was that caused such a deep emotional reaction.

"Your father's name isn't Otis." Otis was the name on my birth certificate. I was in shock.

"What are you talking about and why are you just now telling me this?" I asked.

She continued, "When you were born, a nurse came to me asking for certain information for the state statistical report. She asked the name of the father. I said, Otis because that's what we all called him. But it dawned on me just now that his name wasn't Otis. It's Ceotis."

I said, "There's a big difference between Otis and Ceotis." My mother was crushed and embarrassed.

When I got back to New York, I called Julius and told him the real name. He said what I already knew…that he'd have to start a new search, this time for Ceotis Tuggle.

On April 19, 2005, he called me at my college office to tell me he had found my father and gave me his phone number in Detroit, Michigan. I called the number and a man answered, "Hello." I gave my name and told him I was trying to find my biological father and was following up on a lead. I wanted to know if he'd allow me to ask a few questions. He said I could. I asked if he had ever been to Denver, Colorado. He said yes that he'd been there a time or two. My heart started racing at that point. I asked if he was there in 1947, and he said, "Yes, I believe I was." I got really excited and asked the third question, "Do you remember a gal by the name of Mertis Jean Hawkins?" There was a long pause. I waited. Then he said, "No, I don't remember such a name." I thanked him for his time, wished him a wonderful day, and hung up the phone.

Twenty minutes later, my secretary came to the door and said a woman on the phone insisted on talking to me. I told her to please take care of it.

She said it was important and I should speak to her. I asked her for the name, and she said her name was Mrs. Tuggle. Well, the only Mrs. Tuggle I knew was my wife, and she'd never call me on my office phone so I took the call. The woman said, "Did you just call my house?" I told her I called and spoke to Mr. Tuggle as I followed up on a lead to find my biological father.

"You're trying to find your dad?"

"Yes, mam," I told her.

"Well, you found him." With that, she called him to the phone. As he approached the phone, I heard her say to him, "Come take this phone, Ceotis. This is the boy you've been asking about all these years."

When we resumed our conversation, he acknowledged that he did, in fact, know Mertis Jean, that gal from Oklahoma. I never told him about where my mother was from. He knew already. I literally was at a loss for words. Over the years, I had prepared a speech, but then I was speechless. I asked if I could call him back that evening. Imagine a son finding his father after forty years of searching.

I went into Dr. Sean Fanelli's office, adjacent to mine, and told him what had just happened. He was aware of my search to find my father. He seemed almost as excited as I was. It just so happened that MPC had its annual revival that week conducted by Rev. Jerry Cannon, pastor of C.N. Jenkins Memorial Presbyterian Church in Charlotte, North Carolina. So, I had to wait until the worship service was over before going home to make the call to my "father."

ONE PHONE CALL MADE ALL THE DIFFERENCE

All I could think about that evening was the thought of getting home. Evette was bubbling over with anticipation, so she joined me on the call. When I called, he answered almost immediately. We spent the first part of the conversation with him expressing disbelief that I was so persistent in trying to find him for forty years. He couldn't believe it. Then we got down to discussing each of our respective lives, our families, our children, and more. Then he asked the pivotal question, "Is your mother still living?" I told him she was still living in Denver, but was very sick with stage four cancer. He wanted to know if she'd speak to him. I told him I didn't know, but I'd call and ask.

"Yah, I want to speak to that rascal." She exclaimed. They spoke for more than an hour.

When they finished, I asked mother, "Well, is he my father or not?"

"Oh yeah, he's the one."

"But how do you know? We didn't take the DNA test."

She explained how they asked personal questions that the other should know, so they could connect the dots and recognize each other. They asked about the names of old friends, where they used to go for dates, what my mother's mother looked like, what they used to argue about the most. Then, for the first time in my life, I felt the void was about to be filled. When I called him back he said, "God is good all the time, and all the time, God is good." When Evette heard that, she beamed from ear to ear because that was what I would say to the congregation every Sunday. It was like everything was falling into place.

When I announced these events to the congregation that Sunday, they gave a standing ovation. Evette, Karleena, Lauren, and I wanted to go to Detroit. Regine couldn't go because she was studying marketing in Beijing at the time. My dad flew us out to Detroit for his birthday on May 22, 2005. Upon arrival at his home, we were welcomed with a huge 15 ft. X 20 ft. sign attached on the side of the house that read, "Welcome Reggie and family, with love." Gathered there was about fifty to sixty people, neighbors, friends, and church members. They had converted the garage into an eatery with a large table topped with all the soul food fixins— BBQ ribs, fried chicken, black-eyed peas, potato salad, collard greens, pinto beans, coleslaw, cornbread, pies, cakes, iced tea—the works.

I gave the man I had been searching for forty years a bear hug. Throughout the afternoon, people came up to me to say, "Hi Reggie, I'm your sister, Pat." "Hey Reggie, I'm your other sister, Diane." "Hey brother, I'm Cathy, your other sister." "Uncle Reggie, I'm your nephew, Eric." "Hey cuz, I'm Squeaky, your cousin." "Don't forget me Uncle Reggie, I'm your niece, Erica." This kept on going all afternoon. I met the family I never knew I had, and they gladly welcomed me and my family. I met my dad's neighbors, his church members, his friends. Congressman John Conyers came by the house with a proclamation, the mayor sent over a citation. My dad had been active in the local police auxiliary and was well-known.

The day was magical and way over the top emotionally. I couldn't process it all because it was way too much and too fast.

That night after everyone left, my dad came over to me and tapped my on the knee. "Let's go downstairs and talk."

We had talked only on the phone, never one-on-one, in person. We sat opposite each other. I told him I had to speak first. If I didn't, I'd burst wide open. He agreed. I told him how God has a sense of humor that He waited until we met. I told him I was filled with bitter disappointment for the first twenty years of my search, and I wanted to find him to punch him in the face. I told him how my mother and I lived in an attic for nine years. How I had struggled through college. How it was, not having him around as a child, to go places and do things, like playing ball or fishing, without a dad. How I never got a birthday or Christmas gift from anyone named father. But over time, by God's grace, my rage turned into curiosity and then into a fond desire to simply see my paternal roots. I wanted to know what kind of man was my dad.

"God delayed our meeting until now. I can honestly say I do love you and I respect you," I told him. "I hope we can build a meaningful relationship going forward," I added. All my anger and bitterness was gone.

He listened without interrupting. Then he said, with sadness in his eyes, that he was very sorry, but there was nothing he could do about what he had done. He said he left Denver ten days after my birth. He was too young to be married as my grandmother demanded he do. He didn't want the responsibility of raising a son or of being a husband. Moreover, he couldn't undo anything now. The past is the past. He also said I would not have liked him when he was a young man. He was a womanizer, he drank too much, and he was a gambler too. He was not the best husband or father. None of the children he raised went to college. It wasn't until he turned forty-seven and accepted Jesus Christ as his Lord and savior that his life changed, but by then, the damage he had caused was done. We talked for about an hour. I asked what he would like for me to call him, dad or father. He said he liked "dad." From that night onwards, by the grace of God, we developed a very strong and loving relationship.

When I went back upstairs, Evette wanted to know how it went. I told her about the conversation. She said with some astonishment, "Reggie, don't you see what happened? Don't you get it? He said he left Denver ten days after you were born. That would be April 19, 1947. Julius found your dad on April 19, 2005, that's fifty-eight years to the day. You lost your dad on April 19, and you found your dad on April 19, fifty-eight years later."

Finding my dad was made possible because of all the *69 phone calls. Had Susie Tuggle, my dad's wife not called me back on that fateful day, we would have never connected. She's gone now, but I thank God for Susie (I lovingly called her mother) for her courage to call me back. Many women would not have done what she did. On one of my visits to Detroit to meet dad and mom (Sue), she suddenly got up from her chair and went to the kitchen while we were watching television. She came back with a foot bowl filled with warm water and a towel. She knelt at my feet and washed my feet. I felt so uncomfortable. I looked over at my dad and asked, "What is she doing?" He just shrugged his shoulders and said, "Leave her alone." But that was something she wanted to do. Also, my biological mother and Susie became close friends. They referred to themselves as sisters and talked to each other almost daily. Isn't technology awesome?

NOT MY MOTHER'S HAND, BUT DAD'S

Finding my biological father, after all these years taught me the meaning of grace. My mother, later, used to say to me, "You were angry because your dad wasn't involved in your life, but God took him out of your life to serve His purpose. Think about how your life would have been had he been in your life. You were blessed because he wasn't there." That's how grace is recognized, by looking back. We often say, "Except for the grace of God, there go I."

THE LAST BREATH

As God would have it, I missed my mother's last breath, yet I held my father's hands when he took his. Talk about irony. I had been waiting for the vigil at my mother's bedside for nearly a week as she was in hospice transitioning. We had time to talk for several days before she lapsed into unconsciousness. She talked about so many things, how proud she was for the nobleman I had become and how much she loved me, how much she cared for my sister; Janice, and that she, too, would be blessed in the days to come. She talked about her many blessings, beginning as a child, till her deathbed. My dear friend, Pat, from high school, flew in from Chicago to say good-bye to mom.

I had promised to perform the wedding for a person whom I had baptized as a child. I, of course, had no idea when mother would take her last breath, but I reasoned I could fly out to New York on Friday, perform the wedding ceremony on Sunday and fly back to Denver on Monday morning. As I was driving to the wedding venue, my phone rang. It was my sister. I could barely contain my sadness after hearing the news. I missed my mother's last breath that day, October 19, 2008. I conducted the wedding as though nothing was amiss. I didn't want to bring about any sadness on this young couple's special day. I flew back to Denver the next day and conducted the eulogy a few days later and entitled my eulogy, "My First Friend." Mr. William Holder, an elder at MPC and a dear friend and brother in Christ, flew to Denver to help share my grief and to celebrate her life with me. Rev. Jerry Cannon was there, too. Bill's and Jerry's presence made a huge difference in my moment of profound grief and sorrow. The void my mother left still persists, but greater is the presence of her teachings and her spirit.

Dad and Mother Susie flew out from Detroit to attend the homegoing service. He insisted on helping pay for the cost of the funeral. I appreciated it. During the days and months after the funeral, my dad, Mother Susie, and I talked often, and I visited Detroit a few times. Nine months later, my dad had a massive brain aneurysm. Doctors said it was highly unlikely he'd recover. The blood had caused too much damage to the brain. They could keep him on a ventilator, but he was in effect, brain dead. As the firstborn of his children and upon my Detroit siblings' insistence, Mother Susie called me to ask what to do, should they continue on life support or disconnect? I told her that under the circumstances, I'd vote to disconnect and let God do what He wills. She agreed. I flew to Detroit and waited for a few days, and prayed along with the rest of the family. Waiting in the hospital during times like these is intolerably long. One day after the rest of the family went home. They were preparing to return the next day, so Pat, my eldest sister, and I stayed. Late into the night, in the early morning hours of July 9, 2009, when my dad took his last breath, I was holding his hand. How ironic is that? God, you are amazing! God works in mysterious and ironic ways, His wonders to perform.

Chapter 16

THE PLANS TO LEAVE

F ive years before leaving Memorial, I knew my time there was nearing an end. The signs were clear. I was worn out. For thirty-eight years, I had given myself over to the church and community's service. My life was consumed by meetings, hospital visits, counseling sessions, sermon preparations, Bible study, and other things related to MPC. The church had changed because the community had changed, and I was no longer twenty-six years old. Before my mother passed on to glory, she asked me to slow down and smell the roses. "They smell pretty good," she would say, "but you'll never know because of the way you live."

The congregation was aging, and I was conducting more funerals than my spirit could stand. Those people were not merely members, for they had become like family to me. I had led their children's weddings, buried their parents and spouses, blessed their homes, shared countless meals, and shared their pain and joys. I loved them. Now, however, I was mourning almost constantly. The cemetery visits became more burdensome and emotionally draining. The pleasure of serving the congregation was diminished. People sometimes forget that pastors are human too and suffer the same emotional grief as anyone else. Pastoring is what we willingly do with sincere hearts, but it doesn't come without experiencing profound sadness.

Then, there was the "moving to a foreign country" phenomenon. Moving to a "foreign country" was a term I had coined to describe the large number of people leaving the county to move south to Florida, North Carolina, South Carolina, Georgia, Virginia, Maryland, and Delaware. Every week, it seemed like people were sending notice that they were retiring to a home in the south. This brought on more emotional stress. Even after that, I still had the desire to serve the church and community, but my emotional energy was low. After much prayer and deliberation, I discerned that it was time to move on. The church needed what I could no longer provide. They needed a younger pastor with limitless energy and imagination, who loved the Lord for placing him into that situation. I discussed this new experience I was having with Evette, my sounding board, and prayer partner. We shared our concerns together.

When I came to Memorial in my mid-twenties, the church was small and struggling to survive. Now, it was much larger with thriving ministries, along with being mature in spirit and purpose. I came to a church at a time when the Lord needed someone like me to serve. But decades later, the message was clear that another pastor was needed to carry the MPC assignment to the next chapters of growth. I think pastors can outstay their usefulness, and in doing so, they can harm the church community's health as well. I didn't want to harm the church. I put most of my adult working life into this ministry. It was my life. In fact, perhaps that's the reason why I was born. Of all the difficult decisions I've had to face in life, leaving Memorial was the toughest. I prayed for wisdom on how best to tell the congregation. Over the decades, they had grown closer to me, too. We loved each other deeply and sincerely.

For a couple of years, Evette and I occasionally talked about the day I would have to tell the congregation. I remember anxiously driving to the church that Sunday. When I finally told them, an audible gasp could be heard throughout the church. I said I planned to retire in three years thinking that would give them an opportunity to form a Pastoral Nominating Committee (PNC) and start the process in a decent and orderly fashion. Moreover, Evette and I had to determine where we wanted to live after my retirement. We had a beautiful home in Glen Cove, Long Island, which had to be sold but would've taken time. However, we had no idea it would ultimately take three years to happen.

We kept running into one delay after the other during that protracted time of preparing to depart from Long Island. Finally, one Sunday, a small committee of people came to me and said, "You know you're not going to leave us, right? We've been praying you wouldn't be successful in selling your house. You ain't goin' nowhere!" We all laughed, and I would ask playfully, "What is the name of the God you been praying to, cause my God isn't listening to me?"

Disentangling our lives wasn't easy. Evette was vested in the community in many ways, too. Besides, being born on Long Island, she had created a wide range of interests in several meaningful groups. When I married her, Evette had completed a long and successful career as an executive in the corporate arena. She was then serving as the Executive Director of Business Development for Nassau County and Director of Minority Affairs. At various times, she was the President of the Nassau County Chapter of Jack & Jill of America, Inc., a member of the Alpha Kappa Alpha Sorority, Inc., a member of the One Hundred Black Women of Long Island, and The Links, Inc. Not just that, she was also a trustee at the renowned Friends Academy Quaker School, plus the many lifelong friends she had to say goodbye to. We were engulfed by the process of moving on to our next destination. We were always comparing notes as to how it was going, as we would ask each other, "How's it going? How are you feeling?"

Daily we'd give God thanks that we didn't have to worry about our children. They were all healthy and doing well, prospering in their respective careers. We are so very proud of them all. They worked hard to get to where they are, and they showed their appreciation by being decent human beings—generous, loving, helpful, and pleasant. So, we weren't concerned about how they were doing. They loved the Lord and had the blessed assurance of His protection. However, I could not have moved on in peace without the support of my wife, Evette.

Chapter 17

PREPARING TO MOVE TO A NEW LAND

In Genesis chapter 12, the narrative tells the story of when the Lord said to Abram,

> *"Leave your country, your people, and your father's household and move to the land I will show you."*

S o, Abram left, and the Lord told him, ***"This is a critical event in the development of the Israelite nation."*** Abram's decision to be obedient and leave for a country he knew nothing about was an act of faith. He was relying on Jehovah to protect him and provide for his needs. He was leaving the comfort of his own people, in his own familiar country where he had a position of extreme wealth and a stellar reputation. Moreover, he was also taking his family and servants with him. Had he not obeyed and remained in his comfort zone, Israel's future could have been placed at risk.

I felt a little like Abram (Abraham) when I made the decision. I was well-established, professionally secure at the college, and enjoyed a solid relationship with the folks at MPC. I served on several boards, including a philanthropic foundation. Evette was born in Glen Cove, and while some of her family had moved to Georgia, she still had family and most of her friends on Long Island. Leaving would mean having to reinvent ourselves socially. But it was clear we had to move on. First, I felt I could not live in relative peace because of the lifestyle I lived, having so many social, Church, and political contacts. I (we) felt too exposed. I wanted a more serene lifestyle with fewer meetings and more roses to smell.

Second, there was the notion of living on a fixed income. Long Island is a beautiful place, but the living expenses are among the highest in the country. For example, by contrast, the property taxes we pay now are one-fourth of what we were paying in Long Island. We wanted to travel, and with a lower cost of living, we'd have the additional discretional income to do some of those things.

Third, we wanted to find new things to experience in life. I wanted to write, read at my leisure, go on nature walks, visit museums, play golf, or do nothing at all. I had been over-extended my whole adult life, and now, I wanted to pull back as far as I could.

Our departure from MPC and New York wasn't as dramatic as that of Abram. It's ludicrous to think that any major historical event would be shaped by our moving to Charlotte. Evette and I had to consider many elements with respect to moving to a "foreign country."

In my mind, to retire rather comfortably, five categories before the move had to be addressed. The five elements that all retirees must focus on are spiritual health, physical health, financial health, friends, and emotional stability. After careful review of our lives in all five areas over a couple of years and having endless discussions on how we'd exist in another part of the country, Evette and I felt that God would make it all right for us to move on. Each of our daughters was settled in different states and doing well in their respective careers. Karleena was a successful surgeon in Atlanta, Regine, a respected executive in Bentonville, Arkansas, and Lauren, an award-winning television editor, in Brooklyn. They were all healthy and very much engaged in the totality of life. When our children are all doing well by God's grace, words of thanks constantly flow from our lips. We considered other parts of the United States to move to, but we both agreed on Charlotte.

In 1990, Mildred Brown and Rita Dixon of the office of Church Development at the General Assembly headquarters, organized a leadership conference in Montego Bay, Jamaica. About fifteen of the denominations' strongest African American pastors were invited to attend, including Rev. Robert Burkins of East Orange, New Jersey, and Rev. Charles Heyward of Charleston, South Carolina. All of us were involved in congregations that were thriving and growing. We sat through several advanced seminars on what it takes to move our situations to the next level. Among those attending the conference was Rev. Jerry Cannon, pastor of the Northeastern Presbyterian Church in Washington D.C, at that time. Later, he would accept a call to pastor the C.N. Jenkins Presbyterian Church in Charlotte, North Carolina. From that initial meeting, Jerry and I became close friends and brothers in Christ. We preached at each other's church on several occasions. We would meet each other at different conferences where we would be featured speakers on church growth and evangelism. By a large percentage, most black Presbyterian congregations are small, and many are not healthy enough to call a pastor, either full or part-time. C.N. Jenkins, Memorial, and about five other congregations in the country would be called on to help mentor other congregations on techniques and methods that would lead to church growth.

On one of my visits to preach at Rev. Cannon's Church, some MPC men and our praise dance team accompanied me. Evette and I asked Jerry to show us around Charlotte. From that tour of the city, Evette and I had found the place for our next move. Charlotte met the basic criteria of what we were looking for in our selection. The location would have to be near an airport for us to be able to visit our children on the east coast, a place that had significant cultural activity. We wanted to live in an integrated community. We wanted it to be a place where colleges and universities were nearby as we both enjoyed going to hear lectures from time to time. With those criteria satisfied, we found land in a great neighborhood and built our new home.

Chapter 18

FLUNKED RETIREMENT

hortly after arriving in Charlotte, I was invited to preach at the First United Presbyterian Church (FUPC). They had no pastor. I was invited for several more successive weeks, and then, they asked if I'd serve as their interim pastor for one year. I had nothing else to do, and I enjoyed pastoring. So, with the understanding that I would not seek to ever become their pastor, I accepted the invitation for one year. The Elders had heard of my time at Memorial Presbyterian Church and how it grew from fewer than 40 members to nearly 1000. They were excited to have both Evette and me.

FUPC is a wonderful organization that had a membership of about 120 people, with about sixty to eighty in attendance on any given Sunday. We loved the warmth and sincerity of the people there. It was a much simpler operation compared to MPC and, thus, much less stress. There is a correlation between the congregation's size and the size and complexity of problems; the smaller the congregation, the simpler and less complex the problems. I made myself available for all pastoral functions, preaching, visiting the sick, counseling, officiating funerals, officiating weddings, serving on judicatory committees, representing the church at community meetings, and moderating the monthly Session meetings. I enjoyed it.

As the first year was coming to an end, I was approached by the Session and asked if I'd serve for another year. I was told that the people enjoyed my sermons and my energy. They felt as though their pastoral needs were being met and with no intra-church disputes. People enjoyed coming to church, and that's why I was asked if I'd agree to serve for another year. With nothing else to do, I accepted again. I ended up serving this congregation for four-and-a-half years. They finally called a younger, full-time pastor. He was committed to the Lord and had tremendous energy and imagination to serve. FUPC should do well under his leadership.

Next, I took a year off from pastoring. During that time, I was asked to be the moderator of the New Friendship Presbyterian Church in Huntersville, North Carolina. It was a community about forty-five miles from where I live. I preached there most Sundays, and when I wasn't there, I was invited to preach at other places. One of the sad realities of African American congregations in Charlotte and around the country is that many are too small to conduct the kind of effective ministries they'd like. They are filled with people who love the church and each other, but they struggle because they find it difficult to attract new and younger members. This paradigm is repeated time and again. It's one I know intimately well. MPC was once such a church.

In July 2018, I became the Interim Pastor at the Grier Heights Presbyterian Church (GHPC), Charlotte. It was also a small congregation with approximately 120 members, with about sixty to eighty in church on any given Sunday. It's different from FUPC. Every church has its own unique characteristics. The Grier Heights community is not a wealthy zip code. What makes this fact so astounding is that it is adjacent to Myers Park, one of the wealthiest communities. In fact, the history of Grier Heights is that many of its residents were the domestic workers, and gardeners, and helpers of those who lived in Myers Park. FUPC does not have a well-defined neighborhood community to serve as it is located in the downtown commercial district's heart. By contrast, GHPC is able to better serve its community residents, and it does so quite well. In many respects, I'm in my element. I firmly believe a church must serve the community, its residents, and their needs. The demographics at GHPC are the same as they are at FUPC. The average age is sixty-give and older, which means the physical ability to do more is limited. I think they'd like to do more but time catches up with all of us. The spirit is willing, but the flesh is weak.

I have a major concern about the longevity of many of our local congregations. Unless they are able to attract and retain new blood, these churches' lifespan is on the nearby horizon. It's a shame because the gospel message is needed now more than ever. The social disparities in economics, politics, and social integration are overwhelming. FUPC and Grier Heights Presbyterian will survive, I am convinced. But many of our churches will not. The church's purpose has never been greater, and a need more intense. Of course, the purpose of God will not be stopped, but God uses people to be His instruments of change. The presence of the Presbyterian Church in these communities may be threatened because they are not or cannot provide effective ministry. **God will use other means to obtain His objectives. God will not be placed in a box, and He is not limited to what we do or fail to do.**

You can take the person out of ministry, but you can't take ministry out of the person.

In addition to my serving as interim pastor at the Grier Heights Presbyterian Church. I joined in an effort in 2019 with Rev. Dr. Willie Keaton, a Presbyterian pastor and Rabbi Judy Schindler, a local community activist, to create a 501(c)(3) organization called, Restorative Justice. We did this because we learned that in 1960, the city of Charlotte tore down an economically viable black community to build a highway and high-rise condos. The city council at the time promised to rebuild the community better than before. As it turned out, our creation of this organization was ahead of its time. On May 25, 2020, George Floyd, a black man, was murdered by a white police officer in Minneapolis. Virtually, the entire country was outraged by this heartless act. Protests and demonstrations erupted across the nation along with other parts of the world. At that time, most of the protestors were white. As much as it caused enormous sadness, it also brought on a sense of renewed hope for meaningful change in America's social fabric.

A Harvard study released in 2015 showed that Charlotte ranked last among the 50 cities with similar demographics for upward mobility by blacks to move out of poverty. Fifty out of fifty, the lowest on the list. We set out to challenge this reality. After several meetings with community leaders, city council members, and the mayor, our new organization successfully got the mayor to publicly state an apology on August 10, 2020. The apology was for what the city did in 1960 to the black community. Black leaders told us early on that we'd never get such an apology, but we did. We didn't stop there. We have had additional meetings with the largest foundation in Charlotte and with the mayor. We did this to further create a meaningful plan of action to establish a strategic set of steps that will lead to the elimination of social and economic policies that promote or encourage systemic racism. We want the city of Charlotte to create structures that aid upward mobility for those left behind due to gentrification. So far, we've raised nearly $80,000, including a $25,000 grant from the General Assembly of the Presbyterian Church, $20,000 from the Myers Park Baptist Church, $10,000 from Duke Energy, the United Way, and others. I serve as the board treasurer. Our initial goal is to raise $20,000,000 from the government, foundation, and corporate gifts by 2022. I believe we can do it.

Chapter 19

REINVENTION

There are a host of frightening things that confront a retired person all at once. The notion of re-establishing oneself in a new social arena, apart from the obvious aspects such as having sufficient finances, adequate health, and a sound mind, is critical. After spending more than forty years in New York and being well-known in several communities, we were forced to reinvent ourselves in a new place, a new home, new streets to learn, a new neighborhood, new friends, and new culture. Yet, this is what we actually wanted.

I decided I would not join any organization outside the church. I've had my fair share of meetings, and so far, except for the Restorative Justice organization, I've stayed the course. So how were we going to make new friends? Fortunately, Evette was a member of The Links, Inc. We had met some wonderful people who became close social and personal friends of ours through the organization. Six years ago, she was also elected to serve on the Board of Directors of the Harvey B. Gantt Center for African American Arts and Culture, an exquisite organization that features artists, musicians, historians, and world renowned guest lectures like Dr. Henry Louis Gates, Dr. Cornel West, and Pulitzer

Prize winner, Isabel Wilkerson. We began to establish meaningful relationships through these two organizations. She gained a wide range of friends, and I found some wonderful golf partners who enjoyed playing weekly. At this point, I have as many friends as I need.

Being retired is not how it's made out to be, it's better. I missed my former way of life for about three weeks, then I got used to this new lifestyle, get up at my will, do what I want or not want to do during the day. I can read, prepare sermons, go to museums, etc., anytime I want to. I even go to the gym literally seven days a week, including Sundays, before going to church.

Evette and I go for two to three-mile walks regularly. We have traveled to Alaska and several countries including: Greece, Portugal, Spain, Italy, Russia, Denmark, Estonia, Sweden, Israel, Monaco, Cuba, Singapore, Vietnam, Cambodia, Hong Kong, several Caribbean Islands, South Africa, and more, over the past ten years, mostly via cruise. We enjoy visiting our children as often as feasible.

God's grace is amazing, and the journey through grace is exciting, having more twists and turns than one can predict ahead of time. For me, the secret of a full God-fearing life is keeping the balance between planning what to do and yet, not planning too much. Leaving room for the unknown to happen and trusting God to make something good come into view. We should not develop such complete plans where there is no room for God's grace to manifest itself. We are never in total control of all the events in life. We have to relax in moments of uncertainty and wait to see what God will do. The major challenge in life is to learn to relax in times of trial and tribulation and let God have His way.

On one hand, it's uncomfortable because we have a propensity to force issues in our direction, but on the other hand, it's liberating in the sense that we are released from trying to control events beyond our capabilities. We are not God, so why pretend that we can be? That is the recipe for extreme stress.

This philosophy is reflected in the often-quoted saying:

"God grant me to change the things I can; the courage to accept the things I can't; and the wisdom to know the difference."
—Dr. Reinhold Niebuhr

Thank you for taking this journey through grace with me. I hope it has inspired you and you find reason in your own life to thank God for His grace.

God has smiled on me,
      He has set me free.
God has smiled on me,
      He's been good to me.

After I preached my first sermon in 1963, Mrs. Gray, a deacon at the Macedonia Baptist Church in Denver, Colorado, gave me the following poem by S.H. Payer:

Live Each Day To The Fullest

Live each day to the fullest,
Get the most from each hour, each day,
and each age of your life,
Then you can look forward with confidence and back
without regret.
Be yourself, but be your best self,
Dare to be different and follow your own star.
Don't be afraid to be happy and enjoy what is beautiful.
Love with all your heart and Believe that those you love,
love you.
When you are faced with decision, make that decision as
wisely as possible.
The moment of absolute certainty never arrives.
Above all, remember that God helps those who help
themselves.
Act as if everything depends on you and pray as if everything
depends on God.

CPSIA information can be obtained
at www.ICGtesting.com
Printed in the USA
JSHW040251160421
13629JS00003B/16